# MAKE LOVE EVERY DAY

A New Tantra For The Connected Couple

KATHRYN COLLEEN, PhD RMT

TREND FACTOR PRESS

Trend Factor Press, a division of Sparticle Concepts LLC
1530 P B Lane #M4819, Wichita Falls, TX 76302-2612
KathrynColleen.com

Copyright © 2020 by Amy Kathryn Colleen Messegee, PhD RMT. All rights reserved.

This content is protected by United States and International copyright laws. No part of this content may be reproduced or distributed without the written consent of the author.

ISBN 978-1-7348534-7-6 (paperback, English)
ISBN 978-1-7348534-8-3 (ebook, English)
ISBN 978-1-7348534-9-0 (audiobook, English)

To contact the author, or to find more information, please visit KathrynColleen.com. Your thoughts and questions are welcomed.

Cover Art by Kathryn Colleen, PhD RMT

Kathryn Colleen, PhD RMT

# TABLE OF CONTENTS

## A New Tantric Practice

Experimenting With Tantra
8
Complete Connection (Purna Asatti)
14
Complete Connection To Your Partner
18
How This Extends To All Relationships
24

## The Foundation

Building Trust
26
Building Safety
33
Grounding Each Other
36

## Connecting To Your Partner Through Sexuality

A New Tantra
40

The Experimentation Phase
45
Exploring Levels Of Orgasm
52
The Energy Phase
58
The Divine Phase
62
The 360 Phase (Putting It All Together)
67
Make Love Every Day - An Experiment
70
The Multi-Orgasmic Man (Pinching And Pills Not Required)
78

## Independence and Strength of Self

Reveling In Their Journey
82
Celebrating Their Uniqueness And Strength Of Self
88

## Love, Compassion And Expression

A Practical Definition Of Compassion
94
Games For Love And Compassion
100
Expression
104

## Purpose, Wisdom And Oneness

Understanding And Supporting The r Purpose
113
Creating A Shared Vision Of Your Future Together
119
Encouraging Intuition And Seeing Their Divine Light
122
Oneness And Transcendence
125

## All About Love - Frequently Asked Questions Answered

The Capacity To Love And Be Loved
130
Why We Seek Love And How To Know If Love is "Real"
133
Real Love = Joy, Awe And Gratitude
142

How Can I Improve My Connection To My Partner By Myself?
146
Finding Real Love In An Age Obsessed With Looks
149

## Useful Guided Meditations

Connecting To Your Sexuality - Mind, Body And Energy
154
Connecting To Your Internal Energy And Feelings
160
Connecting Completely To Your Partner
164

## Support For Your Journey

Questions, Answers And Additional Resources
170
About The Author
171

Kathryn Colleen, PhD RMT

# A New Tantric Practice

## Experimenting With Tantra

Let's talk about sex. You cannot sufficiently research and experiment with the enlightenment methods of the world without discussing Tantra. While Tantra, in its origins in India, encompasses a full range of methods and practices for achieving oneness and bliss, western concepts of Tantra are entirely focused on sex. When we think of Tantric Sex, we think of the Kama Sutra, and maybe Sting, who is famous for practicing it.

I decided to give it a go. Having a great suite of methods and practices for my various other chakras, I felt that my root and sacral chakras could benefit from more exploration. In other words, if sexuality and orgasm are a path to enlightened spirituality, it is a path that I had not yet fully explored. Let's do it!

I approached it with the giggles typical of the western mindset. It was all good fun, until I realized there was a lot more here to discover. ...

The focus on rising energy through the body and on breathing appear to be the doorway not only to more intense orgasm but, more importantly, to more intimate love making. More than that, sexual union offers a mechanism for more complete connection across all aspects of your relationship. And that connection feeds the sexual union in turn, spiraling the both of you upwards in increasing connection across your entire existence: physical, mental, emotional, energetic and spiritual.

The power dynamic within the relationship and in the bedroom is just one aspect to experiment with. Don't just think about bondage games here. Power often lies with the feminine as a gate keeper, deciding when, where and how sex will or will not happen. The dynamics of shifting power from all the power in the gate keeper (the yin, or feminine) to a shared power and exchange of energy has brought more respect, love, romance, play and appreciation to our connection and to our daily lives. We will play with this idea later in an experiment I call Make Love Every Day.

In my studies and experimentation, I began where most people would, with the ancient eastern tantric practices. But I have a major objection here. I do not agree with the eastern concept that the male orgasm results in a loss of life force (prana) for the male or yang of the couple. From my own experience, I believe that orgasm, both male and female, is a giving of life force to each other. It is not a net loss for one party, but a giving and receiving. Perhaps each party "looses" life force to each other via orgasm, and the feminine partners simply never had the opportunity, resulting in a net loss for the masculine and a net gain in life force for the feminine.

Eastern tantric writings are male focused. This is understandable given the historical context, but problematic. What I noticed is that male tantric teachers will take a male focused approach centered around prolonging sexual union and ultimately avoiding male ejaculation entirely (due to what they see as the loss of life force). In these teachings, female orgasm is rarely discussed and the feminine is little more than a mechanism, or a partner-in-service to the masculine in this effort.

Enter the writings of Margot Anand. Her tantric sexual practices from the female perspective are entirely different, focused on each individual partner using sexuality, sexual union and orgasm to achieve individual enlightenment, and ecstatic bliss. She also details a full scope program for addressing our physical and psychological roadblocks so that we can achieve this. These physical and psychological roadblocks are important to address if we are to fully let go into the experience. I am so thankful that she addresses these aspects of personal development and self understanding.

(Side note: I absolutely adore her writing. I find that I get lost in her books, voraciously devouring page after page of insight. I cannot recommend her work highly enough.)

Tantric teachers, however, are not the only ones to recommend sexuality as a means of communion with the divine. Many world religions have addressed sexuality. Pope John Paul II said that sexual union between a married couple could lead to understanding, "...the meaning of the whole of existence. The meaning of life." He recommended sexual union as a form of worship and a way to experience the divine or sacred, in his writings in *Theology of the Body*.

One Hadith within Islam suggests that the man should not leave the bed until the woman is satisfied. In Wiccan writings, sexual union represents the union of God and Goddess and is used ritually in some gatherings.

Egyptians even had a form of sexual practice called "Ankhing" that they believed would help lead to each individual partner's enlightenment. Ankhing is the movement of orgasm energies out the back of the heart chakra, to help the energy go up, around the crown and back in through the front of the heart chakra. In their belief, orgasm was not a drain of life force, but an opportunity and a mechanism for eternal life for the individual.

All these approaches, western to eastern, ancient to modern, masculine to feminine, however, are entirely focused on the individual, with the sexual union of two people being used to forward the enlightenment and self-understanding of each individual person. **What I do not see in any work from any culture (so far), is emphasis on the connection between two people; the giving of divine energy to each other (rather than channeling it upwards for themselves).**

What is missing is the idea of complete connection between two people, of the kind that allows both, together, to transcend individual existence and time as a unified whole... a kind of connection across every aspect of your existence that includes deep unconditional love, sexuality, intellectual union, and so much more, each aspect nurturing and supporting the others.

It is time for a new Tantra - one that focuses on a complete connection between two people that includes sexuality as a major component, but goes so much farther.

## Complete Connection (Purna Asatti)

Complete connection between two people is challenging. You have to clean out (or accept) past abuses, attachments, transgressions, regrets, in all forms between you and everyone you have ever had any kind of relationship with. (Parents, siblings, friends, family, lovers, mentors, teachers, etc). Then, you have to create internal space and conditions wherein you are ready and intent on opening yourself up to complete connection.

Sexual connection is easier (we think), because it seems like connection but we can tend to go about it without much actual connection beyond the physical.

Complete connection, in contrast, is connection across every element of our being, which are conveniently enough represented by the chakras. Even if you don't buy into the idea of chakras, they very tidily give us a map for various important aspects of ourselves:

- Root - safety, trust, grounding

- Sacral - emotions, creativity, sexuality

- Solar Plexus - will, power, independent self

- Heart - compassion, love, integration

- Throat - personal truth, expression

- Third Eye - perception, intuition, inspiration

- Crown - wisdom, transcendence, unity

It can be scary to connect even just the heart because all relationships end in pain via death or desertion. To open yourself in this way is to guarantee pain. Or is it? Could complete sustained connection be the key to not feeling the pain of separation, even in death? Could complete connection be the key to an infinite, permanent connection that never separates but just morphs into something more?

It helps, but is not required, to first connect with yourself across each aspect of your being before you connect with another. You must be complete unto yourself, although you might have some baggage still.

Given how the universe is ruled by dichotomy, it makes complete sense that only through complete connection can we transcend separateness and its associated pain.

I think it is time for a new kind of Tantra... A practice whose goal is complete connection to yourself, your reality, and others. Sexuality is one critical component of that, but only one of many.

Enlightenment through connection to self, reality, truth and others - Purna Asatti (from the Sanskrit) - complete connection. To experience the oneness, you have to live the oneness, and there is no oneness without connection.

Complete connection is about seeking and fostering a complete connection to your self (mind, body, spirit, development, life, manifesting, etc), your humanity, your past and future, your life here and now, your money, this moment, other people, places and things.

The oneness or unity that everyone talks about and seeks is a feeling of connection to all things. Love is a feeling of connection to yourself and others. Health, strength and gut instinct come from connection to your body. Wisdom and truth come from connection to this moment. ... You get the idea. It's all about connection.

What do you need to connect with? What would it be to feel connected to that?

## Complete Connection To Your Partner

Few things are more fulfilling than romantic love. So how can we make it even better? Cultivating a complete connection with your partner, I have found, is a gateway to more love, more romance, more play, more fun, more and better sex, and more emotional intimacy. More than that, it is a mechanism to seeing and experiencing the humanity of each other, leading ultimately to both of you evolving further together in your own individual journeys, accelerating each other's efforts.

To cultivate complete connection, I recommend working in order from the ground up to make sure you have a solid foundation and are not missing anything. In the chapters that follow, we will be walking through the following roadmap for connection in detail. Here is an overview of our journey.

**ROOT**

Connect with your partner through trust, safety and grounding.

- Build trust
- Build safety (including bodily autonomy)
- Ground each other

**SACRAL**

Connect with your partner through sexuality, the infinite divine, and the infinite energy

- Experiment, and be honest
- Feel the infinite silence and energy inside each other, allow it to rise and build
- Give of your energy to each other
- Give of this infinite peace to each other

Note: it helps to be at peace when you come to bed so that you can be a place of peace for each other. Think of ways that you can put yourself at peace, or avoid triggers before spending time with your partner.

## SOLAR PLEXUS

Connect with your partner's independent will, power, individuality, uniqueness and strength of self.

- Celebrate their uniqueness and quirks

- Encourage their strength of self

- Revel in their journey, how they enjoy their interests. Take the time to listen without expectation of response.

- Be careful of arrogance and power trips centered in insecurities.

## HEART

Connect with your partner through love and compassion for self and each other.

- Eye gazing, snuggling, hugs, hand holding

- Compassion for current challenges - compassion is seeing their humanity as an aspect of yourself, not trying to solve their problems for them, unless they specifically ask for your help or ideas.

- Play, flirt, give each other time, attention and priority.

**THROAT**

Connect with your partner's personal truth and expression.

- Create an environment between you where speaking your truth is rewarded, praised and encouraged, never judged, but held in love and compassion.

- Play Truth Or Truth - ask each other questions in a private place. No judging. See their answers as an aspect of yourself.

**THIRD EYE**

Connect to your partner's higher perception, intuition, and inspiration.

- Encourage your partner's development of perception and intuition (if that is their goal)

- See your partner's divine nature and purpose. See them as an angel, god or goddess. See the light inside that radiates through them.

- Create a shared vision of a future that excites you both and has space for you both to grow, explore interests, and fulfill your purposes in joint support.

## CROWN

Connect to your partner's wisdom, and to your shared oneness and transcendence.

- Talk about how you think the world works and how the divine works.

- Feel at one with each other. See how you are the same. Feel what it is like to be them, feeling what it is like to be you.

- Experience shared transcendence by opening to each other and connecting completely along all of these aspects that you have now developed.

## How This Extends To All Relationships

You will notice that these guidelines (minus the sexuality component) are equally useful for any close relationship that you could want to maintain or cultivate: family, friends, children, and for some, even clients and coworkers. Why? Because human connection is human connection. Real connection is something we all need. It enriches any relationship and creates deep, meaningful interactions that bring out the best in all of us. While you master these principles with your romantic partner, consider applying the non-sexual aspects of these teachings to other important relationships in your life.

# The Foundation

## Building Trust

Trust is the most crucial element in any relationship. While you might do business with someone you do not fully trust, you will not last long in an intimate partnership without trust.

Trust, once lost, is impossible to rebuild in the same way and to the same depth. You have one shot to get trust right from day one. There are plenty of authors and counselors that work to restore broken trust in close relationships; and many that claim success. But in our human psychology, trust is such a critical foundation that unless the root cause of the problem is now gone, there will always be lingering mistrust in the subconscious of at least one of you. If the root cause of the broken trust is now gone, then it may be possible to build trust again.

For example, if the trust is broken by infidelity, you will have to dig deep to find the root cause. Why did they cheat? What were they looking for? Acceptance? Love? Caring? Adventure? Danger? Are you ready to supply that for them? Has the environment changed?

Trust can be broken by other means as well, because partners trust in a lot of things. You trust that you are the number one priority. You trust that they will do what they say they will do. You trust that they love you enough to be on time, to take time and to focus on you. You trust them to stick to the spend plan month after month and to discuss major purchases. You trust that if they have a problem they are facing, they will bring it to you. You trust that they will be there for you when you need them.

Trust can be broken by a gambling addict who hides the losses, by a partner that sets certain topics as off limits for discussion, or who treats your children as second class because they are not biologically theirs. In these situations, to have any chance of reestablishing trust, you must remove the environment that caused the problem by having total transparency on finances, fostering an environment of open communication and squashing jealousy though serious self work. Then, trust might be restored.

In cases where one partner turned against the other, cases of abuse and harm (physical, emotional or psychological), I hate to say it, and please, someone prove me wrong, you are not going to get that trust back again. This relationship will never be what it was. And that is a good thing. Let it go.

So you see how fragile trust is. But at the same time, how trust is the singular foundation for the entire relationship.

Let's suppose that you have not yet broken trust, or that your relationship is new and just starting to build trust, or that perhaps that relationship has not yet come along and you are smartly thinking ahead to become the kind of partner you want to have. Most partners have what I will call a default level of trust. You trust each other on lots of things but may not have ever discussed it.

This is where trust and expectation get confused. You expect that they will do or not do certain things. You trust that they will do or not do them. Same thing, right? Not exactly. Expectation is a form of attachment. It sets us up for stress and disappointment. But is that the same as trust?

Trust is defined as reliance on or confidence in some person or quality. Expectation is about visualizing specific future actions. Trust is inherently broader. We expect specific actions that validate that trust. For example, I trust that he loves me so I expect that he will demonstrate that by giving me attention and treating me kindly. When he does not give me attention, I fear that he does not love me. Trust is about the quality (love), while expectation is about specific action or inaction (giving attention, not cheating, etc). See the difference?

If you require your partner to fulfill a bunch of expectations in order to maintain your trust, then you have no trust at all. Take a moment now to think about your own relationship. Are there expectations? Can you let those expectations go? Why are those expectations there at all? What is your level of trust?

Trust, in relationships, really comes down to believing that this person would not harm you, whether physically, mentally, professionally, emotionally or otherwise. Trust is a risk assessment. That is why we might trust a stranger but not our parents. Trust is a deeply rooted measure of what risk this person poses to do us harm, or to allow someone else to do us harm. If I trust you, it means I think you are not likely to do me harm and I think you'll have my back if someone else tries to do me harm. If I don't trust you, it means I think you are likely to do me harm in some way, or likely to allow others to harm me. Like all measures, it's a sliding scale. You can trust someone a little, or a lot, or not at all, or you can trust them one hundred percent.

So, assuming that trust has not been broken, how do you build it? That is where expectation and validation are your friend. To build trust with your partner you need to:

1. Drop all judgement and expectation

2. Express your needs and fears

3. Listen to your partner do the same

4. Give and receive support for your needs

5. Give and receive protection / care

It is a lot simpler than it sounds.

First, put your judgement and expectations on the shelf, because you need to be able to speak freely. Then, speak up.

Someone has to go first. Don't assume that your partner can read your mind or that they know all your needs and fears. Be brutally honest, and be kind. Now listen. Do not interpret, just listen and remember. Do not respond. Just listen and make a list of what you hear, on paper or in your head. Catalog their needs and fears.

Once you have both shared your needs, support each other. What is support? We throw that word around a lot. You want your partner to support you, but can you define what that means? How can you support them? Support is really just about finding ways to make sure they get what they need. People are not always good at attending to their needs. That's where a good partner comes in. Knowing what their needs are, you can notice when they are not being met. You can ask how you might help them meet their needs.

For example, if sleep is a major need for your partner, and you notice that they didn't sleep well last night, you can offer a hug, say that you noticed, and ask if they could fit in a nap later. You can offer to take some of their chores tonight to give them a break. That is what support looks like. From your partner's perspective, just having you notice their need will make them more likely to be more kind to themselves today. Being seen is the basis for all connection. The effect of this on your deepening connection to your partner can not be overstated.

Address each other's fears similarly. If you know that your partner has a fear of abandonment, for example, you can make a point to come home when you say you will. If you have a fear of spiders, your partner might be the one to get them out of the house. It's not hard. But the effect on your connection with your partner will be profound.

## Building Safety

After building trust with your partner, the next step is building a sense of safety. Trust is an assessment of risk, and in that sense includes feeling emotionally safe that your needs will be met and your fears abated. Now, safety in the sense of physical safety must be solidified. While emotional safety suggests physical safety, you should not assume that physical safety is a foregone conclusion. Physical safety includes bodily autonomy, and feeling protected from outside physical threats.

Protecting your partner from outside threats should be easy enough. Pay attention to your partner's fears. If they fear any particular outside threat, take it seriously and offer protection.

Bodily autonomy means having command of your own physical space. Different people like different amounts of physical contact like hugs, kisses, touch, and holding hands. It is critical to understand and respect your partner's preferences.

Often, partners find each other, in part, based on how much touch, and what kind of touch they prefer. But make sure you have discussed this. A conversation about the kinds of everyday physical interaction you prefer and how much can be something of an aphrodisiac.

- Do you like surprise hugs?

- Do you like to hold hands?

- Do you like to cuddle?

- Do you like it when your partner touches you in passing?

- Where is that kind of touch acceptable or desired?

- Where on your body, and in what venues?

Your partner, and you, need to know that your preferences are respected. If touch is not OK, even just today or right now, it has to be encouraged to say so, and not a cause for offense.

The same goes for physical autonomy outside of yourself. That is, the safety of your spaces and things. We all have sacred spaces and sacred objects. Your childhood teddy bear, a cherished keepsake from your grandparent, or anything that holds meaning is to be respected and protected as an extension of you or your partner.

Talk about your sacred things, and your sacred spaces. Make sure your partner knows what they are. If you are reluctant to reveal a sacred object to your partner, examine that. Why? Do you fear they will not protect it? Do you fear they would harm it or use it against you? In your reluctance is the key to what you need to work on in the relationship.

Absolute honesty is important here, as in every single aspect we will discuss. Honesty is to be rewarded and praised and never to be taken to mean anything about the other partner. Each partner's preferences are only about them.

The foundation of honesty that you are building here in these early steps is just as important as the understanding you are building of each other. Practice it daily.

## Grounding Each Other

Now that you have built trust and safety with your partner, the next thing on the agenda should be grounding each other. Sometimes, one partner may be dealing with a challenge, while the other is in a more grounded place. But the reality is more often that one partner is dealing with a challenge, and the other partner is dealing with the challenge of an unhappy partner. What affects one partner, affects both. Because none of us wants to see our love unhappy. We want to see our love radiating joy. We are happiest when they are happy.

So we see that it is almost never one partner facing a challenge and the other is perfectly happy. But you might find that one of you is, on any given day, in a better place than the other, calmer than the other, or enjoying more perspective than the other.

Helping your partner is also helping yourself. If you can ground them, they can find their peace and joy, and you will find it too. Partners can ground each other then, allowing you both to find peace and joy through your own independent selves and methods.

So what does it mean to ground someone? It means, in simple terms, to calm them down and put them at peace. I think we all know that just asking them to calm down does not work. It has the opposite effect. So if your partner is a bit spun up, or a lot spun up, what can you do?

First, speak calmly, and peacefully. Move calmly and peacefully. Smile at them. Remind them that you love them. Hug them, if they like hugs, or hold their hand. Communicate peace and calm through every fiber of your being.

Then, listen. Let them vent. Get it all out. Look them in the eyes and do not interrupt.

If you are certain that you can fix the situation, you might offer to help. But some situations cannot or should not be fixed. When a situation must be accepted, instead of fixed, offer compassion. You might simply say, "I'm sorry. That sucks. I love you. What do you need?" Give them a chance to think about what they need. They might need some time alone, or some time with you, or a snack, or a doctor, or a different perspective. Let them tell you, and provide for their needs as quickly as you can.

You probably understand your partner pretty well. For couples that have been together for a long time, you might already know some ideas that would help. What always seems to help? A favorite meal or treat? A walk in the sun? A swim? A cuddle? Maybe a funny movie or other distraction?

You will find that in focusing on your partner in this way, you have also grounded yourself. But more than that you have built trust, safety and grounding all at the same time. Now how do you feel? It feels wonderful to see your partner grounded and feeling better. It feels purposeful and important. Because it is. We are here on this Earth to love and support each other. Nowhere is that more important and clear than in a love relationship.

Your partner, in turn, now grounded, will return the favor following your example. Trust, safety, and grounding swirls in an increasing spiral that strengthens your love and caring. And you can do it every day. Become a place of peace for your partner, and they will become a place of peace for you.

Kathryn Colleen, PhD RMT

# Connecting To Your Partner Through Sexuality

## A New Tantra

Once you have established TRUST, SAFETY and GROUNDING with your partner, then and only then are you ready to connect through sexuality. Sexuality, often associated with the sacral chakra, is an entire playground for you and your partner all to itself.

I assume you have the basic how-to already. So let's talk about what it means to CONNECT through sexuality. You might be expecting some tips and tricks for better sex and there will certainly be plenty of those. But let's focus on connection beyond the physical, through the mechanism of the physical. And let's have a really good time while we do.

If you have done your homework, you have already established open discussions with your partner about what they like and don't like. Keep that going here. What would you each like to have more of? Are there particular moves, locations, or positions that you each favor? Maybe some new things you want to try?

As always, absolute honesty is critical, along with not judging yourself or your partner. Don't feel hurt if they are not comfortable with or interested in trying what you want to try. If you are not interested in their idea, try to find a way that they can fulfill that without you, or in some other way with you.

Sexuality is a natural mechanism for connection between two loving partners. It blends trust, safety, grounding, honesty, exploration and self expression. But usually, when we talk with our partner about sexuality, we tend to focus on ourselves... that is, what we want and what we like and what we would like to try. So how can you use sexuality - a very internal personal experience - to get outside of yourself and connect with your partner?

Some cultures and practices believe that sexuality can be a gateway to transcendence (see eastern and western tantric practices), and even a way to honor and connect with God (see the writings of Pope John Paul II... yes, the pope!). Within these cultures and philosophies are also a number of restrictions. For example, there are recommended ideal positions (such as yab-yum, or missionary). Some also recommend that males not ejaculate for fear of losing their energy. (That escalated quickly!) Other philosophies recommend that males learn how to have an orgasm without ejaculating, so that they may learn to have multiple non-ejaculatory orgasms without draining their life force.

You might notice that nowhere in any of these "tried and true" methodologies do we see a discussion of female orgasm. That is an absolute shame. I am here to change that. Allow me to offer a new tantra. I want to state right now that not only is it important for women to orgasm, but...

- Women can have multiple orgasms

- Women can experience up to five different levels of orgasm

- Male ejaculation does not cause a draining release of some finite life force energy (otherwise, my husband would be dead by now)

- And men can become not only multi-orgasmic, but multi-ejaculatory, no pills required.

That was a lot to declare, but I do so from my own experience. That last bullet, about the multi-ejaculatory man, is not just for teenagers, but for men of all ages. Yes, men in their fifties, sixties and upwards can have multiple ejaculatory orgasms within the same encounter, without the need for pills. There is nothing hotter than when your partner is immediately ready to go a second time. It makes you feel incredibly desirable, which just spirals up your own experience, spiraling up your partner's experience.... you get the idea... fireworks!

How? Because sex is not all physical for men any more than it is for women... it is mental, emotional, financial, energetic, divine and everything else. When all is in balance, sex is amazing. And with practice, it only gets better.

Now that you are properly motivated. Let's talk about what practice might look like. Your ever evolving sexual practice will naturally move through several different phases.

- Experimentation
- Exploring Orgasm

## Make Love Every Day

- Exploring Energy

- Exploring The Divine, and...

- Putting It All Together (The 360 Phase)

As you master these phases, I will make one additional recommendation... make love every day. As for any skill, if you practice every day, you will get really good at it, very quickly. But that's not the only reason to make love every day. Our interest in and enjoyment of sex with our beloved is contingent on everything in life lining up just right. In this way, your libido is the canary in the coal mine. If you don't want to make love, don't... and then explore what is off in your world so that you can improve it. We will discuss this in detail later.

## The Experimentation Phase

A great sexual practice begins with experimentation. That is, experimentation with yourself, solo, and experimentation with your partner. As before, and as always, absolute honesty is key. You may find that you are turned on by things that you are embarrassed to admit. You may find that you are curious about something you are shy to share. It's OK. I am not asking you to write blog posts about it (that's my job). I am asking you to share it with your partner.

THIS is why the trust, safety and grounding that you established before are so incredibly important. You must feel safe and encouraged to be completely honest, knowing that you will not be judged. If your partner is shy to talk about something they want to try, or some aspect of their sexual truth, that is a red flag that you have not established the trust, safety and grounding needed for this exercise. Go back and work on that first.

Experimentation means trying new things. You might try videos, toys, positions, techniques, fantasies, times of day, or different locations. If you think you might like it, try it!

## Make Love Every Day

We are not going to list out here all the things you should try. Why? Because each of you, dear reader, is unique. There is no one position or toy or time of day that everyone will enjoy. Sexual preferences are like music and art. Everyone likes something different.

If you need some ideas, here are some resources that may spark your exploration...

- Amazon - the online retail giant has an impressive selection of sex toys, fetish items, massage oils, and other fun stuff. Yes, it is all right out there and searchable. But for us grown folks, check under the sexual health category.

- Adam and Eve - the original online sexual aid shop. They are known for their plain, brown, nondescript packaging and discreet practices.

- *The Joy Of Sex* by Alex Comfort - this timeless 1972 classic is a great starting point, with lots of position diagrams and other ideas.

- *Love, Sex and Awakening* by Margot Anand - This autobiography follows Margot's journey from her first transcendent experience as she seeks to recreate the magic through tantric practices. Other workbooks and books by Margot Anand are equally wonderful and full of ideas to try.

You might notice that I left out the porn category. While it may offer some motivation, it is problematic on several fronts. First, it is impossible to tell if the women involved are being trafficked, or if consent is genuine. You wouldn't want to inadvertently support sex trafficking. Secondly, almost all porn is male-centered. That is, it is focused on male orgasm (the money shot), and the women involved rarely ever get theirs at any level. Third, there is no real connection between the actors. This all adds up to porn being something you may or may not want to experiment with, by itself, but ultimately a lousy resource for further ideas. If you choose to partake, please ensure that it was made legally.

As you try things, you will find that you like some of them, hate some of them, and will find a few things you simply must have from now on, as well as a few things you never want to speak of again.

Just like trying new foods, some are new favorites, some are truly awful, and most are somewhere between. Be honest with your partner about what you like and how much you liked it, or not. After each experiment, a good cuddle helps the honesty flow as you discuss what you liked and what you didn't like, as well as what, if anything, you would like to keep doing for a while or try next.

This phase of your practice should be fun... well, every phase of your sexual practice should be fun. So don't put too much pressure on yourself or your partner to hurry through a litany of experiments, rushing to some perfect ideal. The ideal will happen all on its own quite naturally.

You will find that you have, in the end, a set of favorite positions, favorite toys, favorite techniques, timing, locations, and so on. You will also find that you will have a new language of sexual communication.

Sexual communication is the phrase I use to describe how we talk to each other during sex - how we tell each other what we want, and how we want it. Sexual communication with your partner might include certain phrases to indicate that you want more of something, or faster speed, harder/softer action, a particular toy or technique, etc.

Couples generally use a mixture of actual known words like simply asking for more by saying, "more." But more might also mean faster, or a particular look and approach might convey that you want to switch to that most loved position now. Toys, positions and techniques might have nicknames. You will naturally hone your sexual communication as you experiment.

Another, critical skill that you will develop in this phase, and improve upon for life, is the art of reading your partner, without words. An important, and much more telling part of sexual communication is what we do not say. It is in the body language and noises that your partner makes. With enough experience, and it may not take much, you will be able to tell when your partner is approaching orgasm. You might respond by backing them off of the peak to extend the experience, or revving them up to the big finale. Ask your partner what you should do in that situation. The most common mistake that male partners make is changing speeds when they think their female partner is approaching orgasm. For male partners, revving up to the big finale is often preferred. But for female partners, on average, the right move at the right pace, with the right pressure, held steady without changing, is the secret to a great orgasm.

You might notice that they make certain pleasure noises when you touch them a certain way, and that indicates that today, this move is THE right move. Paying attention to your partner's noises, body language and words, you become lost in a private world together. See how you are now focused on each other? The enjoyment of your partner's pleasure cannot be overstated. When you love your partner, their pleasure is a massive turn-on.

At the end of the experimentation phase, you will have a full set of favorite positions, toys, techniques, timings, locations and language. You will have perfected reading your partner and responding. And you will be having a really really good time. Simply practicing, you will find your skill level becoming fairly impressive and your enjoyment spiraling up.

Exploration never really ends. Time and experience evolves us and you may find new things to explore later. You have built the foundation for honest and open future exploration. But you will reach a point where you want to explore something else... levels of orgasm. That takes you into the next phase.

## Exploring Levels Of Orgasm

You spent the first phase of your tantric study exploring all the positions, toys, techniques, timings, locations and language that you and your partner were curious about. You have perfected reading your partner and responding. And you are having a really good time. It is time now to explore all the possible types and levels of orgasm that your sexuality has to offer.

Let's get our terminology down for this... I rather like the terminology used in other tantric writings so let's use that. The penis is referred to as the VAJRA. In Sanskrit, that means both diamond and thunderbolt. That word is also used for a ceremonial weapon that looks something like a two headed club or barbell style club. Well... you get the idea.

The Vagina, vulva, uterus, clitoris and everything else is collectively referred to as YONI, in reverence to the generative, creative and divine feminine. These words, Vajra and Yoni, remind us that our sexual organs are not just parts of the machinery, but divine, wonderful, powerful and symbolic elements of our total being through which we can explore our humanity and divinity alike.

For Vajra, there is generally one type of orgasm (that is, one set of muscle spams), but many varying intensities. Orgasm can range from mildly intense to earth-shattering. For Yoni, there are various types of orgasm, each with their own levels of intensity and characteristics. Orgasm, for Vajra, is fairly well understood. But orgasm for Yoni has not, until recently, gotten its due attention.

Let's explore the five levels of orgasm for Yoni. If you have Yoni, you may recognize some of these, and find some new aspirations. If you have Vajra, you may be amazed to find such varied experiences available in the complex and mysterious Yoni.

There are tons of articles online attempting to describe the fascinating range of orgasm available to Yoni. Many descriptions I have found focus on which part to stimulate to induce the orgasm. For example, a clitoral orgasm is defined as an orgasm brought about by focusing on stimulating the clitoris.

Here, I will define types of orgasm based on which muscles are spasming or reacting during the actual orgasm. This is just my own characterization. I encourage you to explore as many descriptions and perspectives as you can find.

1. External - centered more in the vulva and external opening. It is very common, even in foreplay.

2. Vaginal - centered in the interior vaginal walls. This is often what most Yonis think is their first orgasm, at least until level three can be achieved.

3. Cervical - involves spasms in the entire vaginal tunnel, as the cervix "dips" down repeatedly; often includes a shot of energy up through the body.

4. Ejaculatory - also know as the squirting orgasm, this one is centered more in the clitoris, but includes the entire Yoni and most of the lower torso and pelvic area.

5. Full Body - electricity seems to build and release upward from Yoni through the entire body, as every

cell in your existence explodes in simultaneous bliss. This orgasm is so good that, in more intense versions, you might actually pass out for a brief moment, have visions of blissful or divine existence and any number of other experiences.

You might have one or all of these at the same time, or any combination. In my own experience, 4 and 5 rarely happen together, but 1, 2, and 3 often happen on the way to either 4 or 5 as the grand finale. But every practice is different. Sometimes 4 and 5 can happen at the same time, or all five at once.

In this phase, I recommend exploring what triggers different types of orgasms and different intensities for both partners. Radical honesty is key, as always. You might say this is an extension of the exploration phase, but to some extent, your sexual practice is all exploration all the time in every phase.

There is a specific danger here that you might have expectations. Type A personalities are in significant danger of expecting too much from yourself. Not every practice will end with a level five orgasm. That is not the ultimate goal.

The goal, if you must have one, is to connect with your partner and enjoy one of the unique perks of having a human body. Orgasm is just a reward for being in the moment. THAT is what your sexual practice is really about.

Sexual practice is really a spiritual and energetic practice. Is it an exploration of all aspects of being human... the desire to reconnect to the divine, the joy of being in the moment, true love and acceptance, and expression without fear of judgement. Orgasm is the reward for focused attention in the now, on your connection with your beloved. If that doesn't keep you coming back, I don't know what will.

While you are experiencing all the great levels and intensities that orgasm has to offer, practice timing your big finale to match your partner. Simultaneous release is something to be experienced. It can be transcendent.

Having said that, Vajra will have a much easier time, in general, timing release to match Yoni. This is not to put all the pressure on Vajra. Yoni will do well to keep the communication going so that Vajra can time things accordingly. As with everything, you might have the goal of simultaneous release, but do not let there be pressure to achieve that every time... or at all. Pressure is a mood killer. Just experiment and keep an open mind. Enjoy when it happens. Enjoy when it doesn't happen. All good sex is good sex.

# The Energy Phase

Once you have enjoyed the exploration phase, and the various levels of orgasm, your next move is to explore how energy plays into this connection with your partner, and into your experience at large.

Everything in the universe is made up of matter, energy and information. That means that YOU and your partner are made up of matter, energy and information. You spent the first two phases of your sexual practice focused on the matter that is your amazing body and all it can experience. Now, let's focus on the energy.

Within an orgasm is energy moving. The sense of electricity building, the release... this is all energy moving within you. Energy also builds and releases upwards in your partner.

This practice breaks down into three parts: connecting to your own energy, connecting to your partner's energy, and exchanging energy with your partner.

First, connect to your own energy. Even as you sit quietly by yourself, you can feel energy flowing through and around you. While making love with your partner, focus on the sensations of energy moving within you. This is an exercise for each partner, within themselves, while you are together.

As you near a climax, notice how the energy builds in one area, releases and rushes upwards to the crown. Imagine drawing that energy up from the root chakra to the crown with every breath in and see what happens.

When you are familiar with that energy movement, try connecting to your partner's energy. See if you can feel differences in the energy within Vajra and Yoni when they are connected as one. You may be able to also feel energy moving in your partner when you touch them anywhere on the body. Practice. See if you can feel it. As you practice, you will become more sensitive to it and more aware of it.

Feeling your partner's energetic response can be as exciting as feeling their physical response. Imagine sending energy down from the crown to the root chakra and into your partner, or into your partner with your hands. See what happens. Emotions are just energy moving, so you might even like to imagine that you are sending love, joy and caring to your partner.

Once you feel fairly well versed at sensing and working with your own energy, and sensing and working with your partner's energy, it's time to put them together.

Try this...

Imagine energy coming down into your head, down your spine, out the root chakra and into the earth. You are a conduit for the energy. This is the energy of connection. This is the energy of all things. This is the energy of life, and love, of your partner and of yourself.

Now reverse the direction. Pull the energy up from the earth, into the root chakra, up the spine and out the crown. Do not impede the flow. Do not keep it for yourself. All the way up and out.

What energy do you feel in the root now?

Now with each breath in, bring the energy up. And with each breath out, bring the energy down. Up. Down. Up. Down.

Now breathe together with your partner. You can match their breathing without them having to think about it. As they breathe out, sending energy out of the root, you breathe in, taking that energy into the root and up, out of the crown. Then you breathe out, sending energy down and out as they take that energy in through their root chakra, and up and out the crown. Then they breathe out and send the energy back down through their root, into yours, as you breathe in and pull that energy up. Experience this for a moment.

This is oneness. This is the potential of your sexuality... This also takes practice. So keep at it!

## The Divine Phase

Having experienced your partner's physical and energetic magnificence, you will naturally start to suspect they are divine. And you would be right! You will begin to see the god or goddess in your partner. They seem to glow with the light of the divine.

The idea of your inner god and goddess is an ancient one. The divine feminine and the divine masculine are worth exploration. These concepts, however, are easily misunderstood.

We each have, in whatever culture we grew up in, a concept of masculine and feminine. We are handed concepts of what is desirable. And we are handed stereotypes about masculine and feminine. I have not seen one yet that was correct or came anywhere close to expressing the full nature of the divine masculine or divine feminine. Let's reset these concepts now, so that we can see both sides of each.

The concept of yin and yang makes a nice starting point. Yin represents the feminine and Yang represents the masculine.

In the all familiar yin-yang symbol, each is equal. They complete each other, and they are included within each other. The masculine and the feminine are never alone, they are always in balance.

The divine masculine and divine feminine are both within each of us. You may find that you tend more toward one or the other, in the presence of your partner, who tends to the opposite in a way that sees you completing each other nicely. But when you are on your own, you find that the other side comes out more strongly to balance you within yourself.

So, what is masculine and what is feminine. There is a misconception that masculine is assertive or penetrating and feminine is receptive or yielding. I would argue that both have assertive or penetrating qualities and both have receptive or yielding qualities.

The divine feminine can receive from the divine masculine. That is the more obvious state. That could include receiving any number of things. But much more important is how the divine masculine can learn to hold a space open in protective strength for the divine feminine to enter, assertive and expansive in her power. We are not taught this aspect as children but must often stumble upon it in later years. THIS arrangement... this SERVICE to each other... is the key to truly deep connection. Sometimes you hold the space for your partner to enter and express, and sometimes your partner holds the space for you to enter and express.

If you think about it, it is not much different than a well balanced conversation. One person speaks while the other listens, acknowledging. Then the other speaks. Here, holding space means defining a physical and energetic space and protecting it, while the partner enters and expresses themselves fully without fear of judgement.

Why is this so rare? It is not rare at all in healthy conversations. But I see many couples still stuck, missing the key ingredient to see this idea fully expressed in their partnership.

On the one hand, it is common to see the masculine as provider, and the feminine as nurturing. This is an age-old idea. We even rail against it, calling it repressive when all we need is to balance it out.

Yes, the masculine can provide physically. Yes, the feminine can nurture. And yes, the masculine can protect this space. And yes... please... the feminine can choose to enter that space to dance, swirl, expand her energies, and experience her power, both literally and figuratively. And the masculine need not be afraid, but need only be fascinated and in awe of her. And yes, he can nurture her expansion and growth in this sacred space. And all of this takes place simply between the two of you. The bedroom is just one place of such service, protection and expression.

The divine feminine, in her full power is as assertive and penetrative as the divine masculine ever is. This can be intimidating and downright terrifying to the inexperienced. You have to be comfortable with yourself in your own full expression before you can be comfortable with someone else in theirs. As you become older and more experienced, you will find it incredibly enjoyable to relinquish yourself to your partner's divine expression and hold space for them to revel in it... masculine and feminine alike.

In terms of our efforts here, practice seeing the divine in your partner and in yourself. Alternate creating spaces (physical spaces, energetic spaces and emotional spaces), holding and protecting those spaces and then entering those spaces to express yourself and expand your divine nature.

That can mean a lot of things. You might have a room where no judgement is ever allowed. You might have a time when you each get to fully express your wild side. You might honor the divine in each other in all manner of ways. Get creative! Read up on these ideas and see where it takes you. Most importantly, nurture your own divine nature through personal development, and encourage your partner in the same.

## The 360 Phase (Putting It All Together)

First, you focused on your own physical enjoyment, and that of your partner. Then, you focused on orgasm specifically. Then, you focused on your energy and your partner's energy. And lastly, you explored the idea of the divine within you both and how you can each hold space for and nurture that aspect. Let's put it all together now.

Each element is there now: physical, energetic and divine. You see and understand your partner on a deep level and on a high level too. You can read and interpret their every sound, breath and movement. You can sense when to hold space and when they are holding space for you. You each express yourself and are growing into your own full humanity and purpose.

Yes, it is about all these things. Sex, now, is about a LOT more than sex. Sex can be a practice field on which we connect to our partners and become ourselves.

The practice, in this phase, is to put it all together: the physical, the energetic and the divine. In your time with your partner, take moments to enjoy your physical sensations and theirs, your energy movement and theirs, fully connected energy (as seen in the previous exercises), and to spend some moments reveling in the divine.

For a challenge, allow your own divine nature to experience this connection through you both. You, as divine, experiencing the physical and the energy, and experiencing your partner's divine nature. Surrender in the moment to your inner god or goddess. Witness the dance... Shiva and Shakti... the divine reveling in being human, seeking to understand itself, divided to experience becoming whole again... joy, love, and connection.

Wow! That's a lot to keep track of. But no worries... The ability to focus on all three (physical, energetic and divine) at the same time comes naturally. First, you focused on the physical. Then you added in the energetic. Then you added in the divine. I will bet that you never really ignored the physical. It was always there. Instead, you built each new skill on the others.

The key here is not a doing, but an ALLOWING. It's about getting out of the way of the experience, allowing the divine to move through you, allowing the awareness of physical and energetic and divine all at once. Don't try... just allow the natural evolution of your practice to happen.

# Make Love Every Day - An Experiment

As you explore connecting to your partner through sexuality, I want to recommend a fun experiment.... make love every day. Some of you are cheering. And some of you are thinking that sounds like a lot of work. This experiment can actually have some very surprising results. Here is my own experience...

**How It All Came About**

You've got to have your priorities. We always spoke about how our relationship and our connection are the most important things in the world. But work gets in the way and kids need attention and .... excuses. And the next thing you know, you are making love only half as much as you used to, and that's not nearly enough.

We missed the connection. We missed the exchange of energy. We missed that time to focus just on each other in an incredibly connected way. And one day, we just decided enough was enough. If our love making was so important, why was it not a higher priority? Why was it not something we made sure happened? We decided to try making love every day, no excuses. Just do it... as they say.

**Finding The Time**

So, what time of day should be our sacred time? At night, after the kids go to bed is the most obvious time. But we were often too exhausted from the day to make love at point. We could give it a go anyway, but it really deserves our best effort. We thought, if it is the most important thing we can do each day, shouldn't it be the FIRST thing we do each day?

Whatever you do first each day is almost guaranteed to happen. That is why some people workout or meditate first thing in the morning. Besides, we have more energy in the morning. And we had noticed before, that any day that began with making love, had always been a good day, no matter what happened at work or otherwise.

Could we, just by making love first thing every morning, guarantee a good day every day and closer connection too? It was worth a try. So we chose the morning. And that meant getting up thirty minutes earlier to make it happen.

## Getting It Done - Embracing The Quickie

Look, we were not about to get up an hour early... because sleep is a priority too. So.... we will just have to get it done, and get it done quickly, but well. Now, IT is defined as he gets his and she gets hers. It is not done until everyone has a satisfactory orgasm. No one-sided experiences here.

And herein lies the interesting question.... if you could have an amazing, mind-blowing orgasm in five minutes, would you still desire the epic hours-long love making sessions we see in the movies? Well, let's just say we both appreciate efficiency. And efficiency is what we got.

## Practice Makes Perfect

You see, any skill you practice daily, you will MASTER. We quickly narrowed in on the perfect positions, techniques and other features that would get us both to a beautiful orgasm in the most connected way, while maximizing for the greatest possible orgasm for both parties.

Now, it's not all about "the O". The important part is connection: emotional connection, intellectual connection, energetic connection, divine connection, and so forth. The playground of sexual intimacy is a space for that to happen. So it's not all wham-bam-thank-you-ma'am. The challenge of a high quality love making session in less than thirty minutes is not for the faint of heart. But we were equal to the task. The practice evolved, over several months to the perfection it is today.

## Don't Forget The Cuddle

Part of that perfection is the incredibly important post-coital tenderness... the cuddle. A good cuddle (especially as an ending to great sex), lowers cortisol levels, boosts the bonding hormone oxytocin, and locks in the emotional connection that you just strengthened.

The danger here, is that you might fall back asleep... actually you are almost guaranteed to fall back asleep, especially if you are waking up early to make it all happen. We learned to set a second alarm that would serve as the final, "get your rear out of bed" alarm. Problem solved.

## The Canary In The Coal Mine

The thing about sex is, it's a great indicator of your total wellbeing. If you have access to good sex, and you don't want it, something is wrong somewhere else in your life. Our rule has been, if one of us doesn't want it, we don't do it... obviously. But that then triggers the critical need to uncover WHY.

It could be something as simple as one of us is sick. Or maybe we did not get enough sleep. Maybe we are stressed out about something. Or maybe we have an issue in the relationship that needs to be addressed. It forces us to examine what is wrong and fix it TODAY.

When you don't let an issue go, you don't let it grow. That makes so much sense it rhymes. When you fix issues quickly, you don't have issues.

The thing is, for many people... and maybe you are one of them... libido is the FIRST thing to go. All the parts of your life have to be in relatively good standing in order for you to desire sex. That's great. Use it as the canary in the coal mine.

The minute your libido goes flat, figure out why and fix it. It is not that your libido is more important than all those other things like finance, work, relationships and such. It's that those other things are important and your libido is the indicator of whether they are OK or whether they are not OK and you are ignoring the problem.

## The Effect Of Guaranteed Sex

So what happens when you are guaranteed to get sex every day? You might think that you wouldn't work so hard for it. You might think that maybe your partner won't work to curry your favor anymore. You might think that you and your partner might give up on keeping your bodies in shape, or you might stop bothering to have date night, or dress nicely, or bring flowers, and so on. You might think you would stop flirting. Why bother, if you know for a fact that you are guaranteed to get some?

As it turns out, the exact opposite is true...

One of the surprising effects of making love every day has been that we actually seem to work harder to be attractive, flirt, and otherwise spin each other up. It is completely counterintuitive. This seems to stem from two reasons. First, we want to be worthy of all that nookie. We both want the other to be excited to make love. We each want the other to be so attracted that every day sex is a joy and a blessing.

Second, when you remove the question of whether sex will happen, when it is guaranteed, flirting is then just for fun. Dating and wooing is just because it's a good time, and you love each other.

There is no longer an expectation of something at the end of the date. There is no worry of getting the evening just right. You relax. You have fun just being together. You connect as people in love. Sex is detached from the dating and flirting and wooing part of the relationship. As a result, the dating and flirting and wooing does not disappear, but flourishes in the absence of pressure and expectation.

Over the long term (months to a year and more), you might think that things would get old and boring. But quite the opposite happens. A good orgasm never gets old, especially when you keep improving your skills and those orgasms keep getting more intense and amazing. So don't worry about that. You can always rotate through different positions and spice things up with various toys, and so forth to keep it fresh and even surprise your partner sometimes.

Lastly, making love every day, keeps your relationship and your connection at the top of your mind. Your connection becomes the clear priority it was meant to be. As such, you find yourself seeking out even more time together, conjuring up romantic surprises, and being more understanding and loving all day long.

# The Multi-Orgasmic Man (Pinching And Pills Not Required)

But let's talk about what I know you all want to talk about... The multi-orgasmic man (pinching and pills not required). It is well known that Yoni is capable of multiple orgasms of various types within the same sexual encounter. Vajra, as it turns out, is capable of amazing wonders too.

I am not referring here to the ancient practice of pinching off male ejaculation in a bid to orgasm again later. I am talking about men of any age enjoying multiple ejaculatory orgasms, just as nature intended, potentially within minutes of each other, without the need for a break, or pharmaceutical intervention.

So how do you get there? This is a practice. Follow all the steps I have outlined previously. Start with physical exploration, exploration of different levels of orgasm, exploration of energy movement, and exploration of the divine within each other. Then, make love every day.

The psychology has to be in place here. Make an effort to ensure that your world is as stress free as possible. Don't criticize each other. Instead, encourage what you DO want. Tell them what was amazing and wonderful. Tell them what was awesome. Tell them how amazing THEY are. You will get more of what you praise and reward.

Don't have expectations. Not every day will be a multi-orgasmic day. Life and circumstances intervene. Good sex is good sex. Don't get all type A about it. Let it be what it will be; no expectations and no pressure. Desire only to connect deeply with your partner.

Keep your bodies strong and healthy. We are asking a lot of these amazing bodies and they work a lot better when we feed them the right food, and tend to our needs for movement. If you take care of your body, you will feel attractive and that only helps the psychology.

So, I hear you ask, does that mean that a chronic condition might spoil our quest? Nope. It is all ultimately in the mind. If you and your partner feel sexy, and feel the connection, I believe you can get there.

Just know that with practice, it is possible. Just be in love. Just be in awe of each other. Let your inner Shiva and Shakti come out. And then one day... once will not be enough. And when that day comes (pun intended), praise your Shiva for the amazing, divine masculine that he is. Allow this unfolding exploration of your humanity and divinity to take you to places that you might not have expected.

Kathryn Colleen, PhD RMT

# Independence and Strength of Self

## Reveling In Their Journey

We are all unique individuals. But in our quest for validation, we seek the company of those who are, in our perception, just like us. There comes a time, therefore, in any relationship when independence and strength of self is tested. The push for independence in a relationship can be the end of it, or it can be an opportunity to take the relationship to the next level of connection.

Independent will, strength of self, individuality, and similar traits are associated with the solar plexus chakra, just above the belly button.

At this point, you have already connected to your partner in terms of trust, grounding, safety and sexuality. You may even be deep into a tantric practice, learning about and celebrating your physical self, energy and divine nature.

Now it is time to focus on what is truly unique within each other. It is time to connect to your partner's independent will, power, individuality, uniqueness and strength of self.

This includes:

- Reveling in their journey and how they enjoy their interests

- Celebrating their uniqueness and quirks

- Taking the time to listen without expectation of response, and

- Encouraging their strength of self

Sometimes we can think we are in love, when really we are just in attachment. Your partner represents something to you. Maybe they make you feel a certain way. Maybe they validate some aspect of you by mirroring it back, or so you think. We can fall into a trap of projecting all manner of attributes onto our partners, and then expecting them to fulfill them. It is time to set all of that aside.

You and your partner are unique individuals, each on your own path, learning about yourselves as much as you are learning about each other. You are both constantly evolving beings, walking your separate journeys together.

## Make Love Every Day

The joy of discovering your partner is not to be understated. But in truth, it is not YOU that is discovering your partner. It is your partner, who is discovering themselves, and sharing that with you, while you discover yourself, and share that with them.

First, revel in their journey. Take joy in how THEY enjoy their hobbies and interests. Some of these will be your interests too. Some will not. Encourage them to do the things that they love to do; the activities that light them up and fill their soul.

In fact... insist on it. You see, we are so wanting to please our partners that we may not all speak up for independent time to pursue our own separate interests. So make sure your partner has the time, space and opportunities to pursue what they are passionate about, separate from what you are passionate about. Why? Because this is the gift of freedom and true support.

Opportunities will come their way. Some of those opportunities may take them away from you for a while, or may take their time and attention for a while. Don't become covetous of them, of their time, or their attention. Quite the opposite; if it is an opportunity that they truly want to pursue, you should find a way to support it. Don't ask, "Why do you want this?" Instead ask, "How can I help? What can I do to support you? What do you need to make this happen?"

Obviously, if your partner is indulging in self-destructive behavior like abusing drugs or criminal activity, you may not want to support that. We all have showstoppers - things that would make us leave a relationship. It's OK to go. In fact, sometimes, it's better to go. You cannot change other people. You can only change yourself. So if you cannot meet them and support them where they are, go somewhere else and free them to live their life their way. THAT is an act of love.

Many partners feel fear around the idea of their love spending time on something that does not involve them. If you feel fear, examine it. If you find that you wish they would not do that activity or take that trip, or pursue that opportunity, ask yourself why. Keep asking yourself why until you get to the truth... you are afraid that.....what?

Are you afraid they will leave you? Find a better partner? Realize that you are unworthy? This stems from you yourself feeling that you are lesser or unworthy. In that case, it would be useful to work on the Stage Six exercise of breaking your own perception of unworthiness. See the book *Purna Asatti* for details on that exercise and a complete roadmap for your own focused personal development.

Resist the urge to control your partner. This will only lead to an eventual end to the relationship. You cannot control another person for very long without building resentment, distrust and misery. This is attachment, not connection.

Are you afraid they will get hurt? Maybe what they want to do is dangerous, relatively. I say relatively because even driving to a desk job is dangerous in its own way. Even staying in your house is dangerous to a degree. Nothing in life is without risk.

Try to understand, through honest conversation, why your partner wants to do what you see as dangerous. Discuss the known dangers. Discuss your fear honestly. Ultimately, however, YOUR fear should not factor into THEIR choice, and your fear should not stop you from supporting their choice with everything you can muster. The key is... their choices are about them, not you, and your fear is about you, not them.

You think you are afraid for their safety but what you are really afraid of is being alone, or being without them. See? Your fear is really about you. It shows you that you have some attachment here that needs to be released and replaced with connection instead.

## Celebrating Their Uniqueness And Strength Of Self

Separate from your individual passions, you each also have a set of unique characteristics and quirks. You may not like some of your quirks. But your partner may find them charming and lovable. Likewise, your partner is sure to have some unique characteristics and quirks that you adore as well. Celebrate each other's uniqueness.

Now, there may be some unique aspects of your partner that are not your favorite. They might have some annoying habits or traits. We all do. You do too. If you focus on those traits, they will grow from annoyance to showstopper and will spell the end of the relationship.

Instead, focus on the traits that you love. These might be traits that you both share, or traits unique just to them. Point out those little quirks that you love. Express why you adore that about them. Tell them why they are amazing. This lines up with the key ideas of Joy, Awe and Gratitude. In everything you do together, or apart, express your joy, express your awe and express your gratitude.

In this case, you are focusing your joy, awe and gratitude on their unique traits, quirks, and independent interests. When it comes down to it, we are all just human. We offer up more of what we are rewarded for. Joy, awe and gratitude are powerful rewards. Offer them to your partner for all their amazing traits, preferences, hobbies, and quirks, and those amazing traits will grow all the more amazing indeed.

A key ingredient in understanding your evolving partner is listening, without expectation of responding. Listen, instead, to simply understand. Encourage them to express themselves; to recount their new discoveries about themselves, their new ideas and preferences.

Understand that these will change over time. We all do change over time. And whatever they may have discovered about themselves and their path in this life, simply acknowledge it.

If they are sharing their joy, be in that joy with them. If they are sharing their pain or frustration, offer sympathy and caring. Your opinion is not always required. A solution is not always necessary. More often, what we seek from our partners is just acknowledgment of our situation and validation of our feelings about it. If they ask for your opinion or for help formulating a solution, then by all means, offer that. But be sure about what they are seeking here, before offering up interventions.

Strength of self is your ability to figure out what you want, or don't want, feel or don't feel, agree with or don't agree with, to express that openly and with confidence, and to speak your truth no matter what. Wow. Now that we defined it, strength of self is a lot harder than it sounded at first.

Many of us here on this Earth struggle to develop strength of self. We fall prey to the opinions of others, doubt ourselves, doubt our truth, or worse, don't even take the time to sit down and really think about what our truth is to begin with. As you and your partner walk along your independent journeys of self understanding, you will work to improve your own strength of self. Encouragement from a loving partner can go a long way in helping us to build that strength.

When your partner is expressing their truth, reward it. What is your truth? Your truth is...

- Any facet of your current self,

- Your past history as you saw it,

- Your future as you want it to be,

- Your past or present feelings,

- Your desires, dreams and goals

- And so forth

No one else can know these truths but you. They are internal to your experience. When your partner expresses their truth, reward it with joy, awe and gratitude. Encourage that expression.

But what if they are expressing something they are not proud of? You are not rewarding the truth itself. In fact, do not judge their truth one way or the other. They are certainly not looking for judgement. You are rewarding the confident expression of the truth. You are rewarding them for OWNING their own truth, and speaking it out loud. That non-judgement and that encouragement to own it and speak it out loud to you, builds their strength of self. It builds their willingness to speak their truth out loud again, with you, within the safe, grounded space of your loving relationship. They know they will not be judged, so they will speak freely. And you can do the same.

Now let's talk about how vulnerability fits in here. If only one of you is sharing your truth, and the other is not, this will backfire by breeding mistrust. There has to be a give and take of personal truth. They share something. Then you share something, and so on. There is a subconscious expectation of reciprocity when it comes to sharing your personal truth with your partner. Doing so increases trust, grounding and emotional safety. Share and share alike. As you listen to and acknowledge your partner's truth, offer some of your own, allowing them to support you in turn.

Kathryn Colleen, PhD RMT

# Love, Compassion And Expression

## A Practical Definition Of Compassion

Having established trust, safety, grounding, sexual connection, independence, and strength of self (wow, that's a lot!), it's time to connect to your partner through compassion and love. As you might imagine, compassion and love are associated with the heart chakra. When you feel love, or when you feel compassion, you physically feel it in your heart. Your heart feels bigger. If you focus on that space in your body, the feeling grows.

It is time to connect with your partner through love and compassion for self and each other. That starts with compassion; specifically, it starts with compassion for yourself. Why? If you are not able to offer yourself compassion, how are you supposed to offer compassion for your partner?

That being said, compassion is a word that is used often, but rarely defined. Let's define it now. From the Latin, it breaks down it into the concept of "suffering with", or shared suffering. That implies that your partner must be suffering, and because they are suffering, you take on that suffering yourself and you both suffer together. After all, misery loves company.

There are a couple of problems with this definition. First, compassion should be possible at any time, without anyone having to suffer. You should share in your partner's joy, too. Second, you cannot cure someone else's suffering by suffering yourself. So suffering together is not exactly what this word was meant to express.

What do we really mean? When we are having a hard time in this life, the ultimate suffering comes from feeling alone in your challenge. Likewise, when we are enjoying a triumph, but we are not able to share it with anyone, it takes all the joy out of it.

When we say that we want compassion, what we really mean is that we want someone else to see us. We want to be seen and we want to be heard. We want them to understand what we are feeling, but we don't always want them to feel it.

So here is a better explanation. Compassion is seeing their humanity as an aspect of yourself. When you see their humanity, you see their quirks, their uniqueness, but also their sameness. They are much like you. They are on the same path as you. They make mistakes, have triumphs, learn about themselves, learn about life, ... just like you.

Their current situation, challenging or joyous, is a situation you have been in, or could be in one day. You see them, and you listen to the details of their experience. You ask for more details. You imagine yourself in that situation. And you acknowledge what they feel as something that you might feel too in that situation. You send them love, in hopes that your love will ease their suffering, or help them find balance, or even that your love will strengthen their joy.

You are not trying to solve their problems for them, unless they specifically ask for your help or ideas. You are loving them exactly where they are, in their current experience, as they are feeling whatever they are feeling, as human. That is compassion, as we will define it here.

Before you can cultivate compassion for others, you must first cultivate compassion for yourself. This may be harder than it sounds. Of course we should love ourselves. Of course we say we do. Of course we should have compassion for ourselves. Right? But somehow, sometimes, it is easier to have compassion for others.

Here's the problem. If you see yourself as lesser or unworthy, you are not having compassion for yourself. To have compassion for yourself is to see your own humanity, to listen to yourself, and to love yourself in your current situation. But it is all these things, while at the same time seeing it all as just one aspect of yourself.

You see, when we have compassion for others, we see them, in their humanity, as an aspect of ourselves... one part of us, not the whole. As they say... no one thing is everything... everything is everything. To see your current self in your current situation as an aspect of your total self, is to see that you are bigger than this one experience.

So in having compassion for yourself, you are acknowledging your current experience, and seeing it as part of your total human experience, not the whole of it. You are making yourself bigger. You are expanding to see your entire humanity, and this experience is one little part. And it is all beautiful and worthy of love that may heal, balance and bring joy. That makes suffering dissipate as you see that this one experience is not the totality of your life, and it keeps your head down to a reasonable size as you see that this one triumph is not the entirety of your existence either. Do THAT for yourself first.

Now you are in a good place to offer compassion for others. Now you can see, hear and acknowledge their current experience as part (or a potential part) of your own, AND as just one part of their entire human experience. You just made them bigger. That is, you saw THEIR entire humanity, and this is one part, and you see YOUR entire humanity, and this is one part.

And here you are, the two of you, sharing the perspective of this experience, no longer consumed by this one experience. The experience is put into its place in the enormous puzzle of your lives. And you realize that in your expansion and larger perspective, you are no longer suffering.

The expansive nature of compassion has gently walked you out of suffering, through the garden of perspective, and now you are standing at the gates of possibility. What will be the next experience?

The practical application of compassion looks like this... when your partner is recounting their day, look them in the eyes. Listen, without formulating a response. Just listen to try and understand what they experienced, whether it was triumphant, mundane or challenging. It doesn't matter. See their experience as one you may have encountered before, or might encounter in the future. Acknowledge the feelings they had. Imagine what you might have felt. And then zoom out from the experience to see it in the grand scheme of their life, and yours. Wonder together about what experiences might come in the future. Imagine good things. Be in joy together.

## Games For Love And Compassion

We get so busy. Sometimes it pays to take a little time and focus on each other. For most couples, that means maybe going out to dinner, or watching a movie. But you can be together, sharing a meal or a movie and never actually connect.

So here are some games to play that will boost your connection via compassion and love. Unlike other games, these can be played by just one of you and still have a good effect. So if your partner is not necessarily into relationship building, you can initiate many of these activities and still get the benefit for both of you.

### Eye Gazing

When your partner speaks, or even when they are not speaking, look them in the eyes. Look deeply into their eyes, like the pupil is the window to the soul. Try to see their soul. This can feel very intense. You will discover that every human on this plant is preprogrammed to respond to this kind of fully concentrated eye contact.

If they are uncomfortable with someone seeing their truth, they will break gaze quickly. This could be because they don't want you to see the truth of their soul, or it could be simply that they feel unworthy of that kind of connection. Obviously, don't do this for too long with strangers, or it will come off as creepy and invasive.

Yes, look people in the eyes when you meet them and when you speak with them. But don't hold the gaze for too long or you will make them uncomfortable. It takes a little trust to allow someone to see your full truth. Start with short gazes during conversations and work your way up to sitting silently, staring into each other's eyes and not saying a word. You will find yourself feeling deeply connected, fully seen, and smiling wildly.

## Snuggling, Hugs And Holding Hands

Sustained body contact increases the bonding hormone Oxytocin, and is a wonderful way to send love and compassion without needing to say a word. Snuggling, hugging, and holding hands all include sustained physical contact and will do the trick.

Now, this is important. Everyone has different personal preferences when it comes to snuggles and hugs and holding hands. Everyone has an ideal amount. If you exceed the ideal amount, they will feel smothered. If they don't get enough they will feel lacking. See if you can find each other's ideal level of contact and fulfill it, without exceeding it.

## Play and Flirt

Ensuring that your partner feels your love and compassion doesn't need to be so serious. Playing and flirting goes a long way. You might call it opportunistic harassment... with permission, of course.

For example, as your love walks by, you might reach out and touch them playfully. A playful poke, pinch, swipe or pat in a prime location, or a kiss on the head or hand when they least expect it shows them that they are on your mind and they are a priority. This is opportunistic attention, founded in joy. Love SHOULD be fun. So look for opportunities to play with light touch in this way.

## Send Love

For an extra challenge, imagine sending love each time you look at your partner, and each time you touch them. Focus first on your heart when looking at or talking to them. Then imagine sending love through your gaze, or down your arm and through your fingers in your touch. Imagine love flowing from your heart, to them, riding like music on a radio wave. Note their reaction. When you hug them or snuggle them, send love. Engulf them in love. See what happens.

## Count The Ways

A fun back and forth game is to tell your partner why you love them, and why they are amazing. Take turns telling each other about all your amazing traits, quirks, and attributes. Hearing that you are awesome never gets old. It makes you both feel wonderful.

Life and love should be fun. Come up with some other games of your own and enjoy this connection as it deepens.

## Expression

The next item on the list for connection is your partner's expression, and your own! As always, you will have a hard time appreciating and encouraging someone else's expression if you cannot appreciate and encourage your own.

So what is expression? Expression, associated with the throat chakra, includes all the WAYS that you convey things to others and the world...

- Verbally - through writing, speaking, and questioning

- Your appearance - through the way you dress, wear your hair, tattoos, piercings, makeup, and jewelry

- Your movement and body language

- Your attitude, energy and feelings

- Even your exploration of your divine nature

You could be expressing all kinds of things: your truth, your opinions, who you are, what you do, what you want, what you think, your dreams and aspirations or anything else. It all mixes together to make up your full expression... your unique self carrying out your mission.

Strength of self comes into play here in that you need to feel confident in expressing your truth. That being said, your expression may include times when you choose NOT to express yourself. There are times to be out loud about something and times to just listen and receive. True confidence in expressing yourself shows when you, at times, choose not to be the center of attention, and at other times choose to shout. The important thing is that it is all by YOUR choice, not because you feel forced, coerced, suppressed, oppressed, or otherwise sidelined.

There will certainly be times when you may choose to express only part of yourself. Often at work, we might only show our "corporate side." At certain gatherings, we might forgo showing tattoos. You get the idea. We dress mostly in line with the standards of whatever situation we find ourselves in. On our own time, we may be more expressive.

While you are beholden to other people for jobs, money, opportunities, and such, this is a good idea. Are you being inauthentic? I hope not. You don't need to be. Out of the dozen facets of your authentic self, you are just choosing to present and use some of them, and save others for other situations.

Does that mean you are suppressing your full self? Yes. Socially, until you are financially independent, you are. The parts you choose to present at work are authentically you. The parts you choose to present at the yoga festival or the motorcycle rally are also authentically you. You are varied and fascinating and evolving.

Once you are financially independent, you will have little reason to hold back any part of your expression because you won't need anything from anyone. See my writings on financial independence, and writings from other great authors for more on the financial side. Suffice it to say that it is entirely possible to get there. This is when your artistic, wild, shamanic, or activist sides will really get space to expand in their expression. Until then, the weekends and days off will suffice.

The one person who will hold you back the most from your full expression is YOU. Ultimately, your expression is your choice. You choose how you want to dress, how you want to wear your hair, how you speak and what you speak about, and so forth. It is ultimately your choice. If you are choosing not to speak up, when you think you should, if you are choosing to dress differently in your free time than how you would like to, or if you are avoiding showing any aspect of your current truth to your partner, that should be examined.

Be careful not to blame your partner for your own unwillingness to express yourself. If they belittle you or otherwise discourage your expression, that is a signal that they are not the right partner for you. It is not a signal that your expression is wrong. You see, in this life, there is no "wrong" expression, just like there is no "wrong" human. There is just massive variety. You should feel free to express yourself in any way you feel like: dance, sing, paint a picture, paint yourself, speak up, speak your truth... Support your own evolving expression and live it.

Then you will be in a good place to support your partner not just through words, but through example. You see, it's hard to tell someone that they should express themselves, when you don't allow yourself the same privilege. Revel in your partner's expression. Encourage them to speak their truth, as before, and now expand that to reveling in all of their nonverbal expression too.

The challenge comes when our partner's expression evolves, and when our own expression evolves. Let me explain. We are always evolving. Over the years, we learn and grow, exploring new facets of ourselves, and the world. You and your partner have gotten used to the way you express yourselves. It's comfortable.

Now you want to express yourself another way. Maybe by some art form, or some new experiences, or some new way of dressing. You worry how your partner will accept that. Your partner worries the same thing as they change over time. Ideally, you can build an environment where you and your partner feel free to express yourselves AND to evolve how you express yourselves over time; where the evolution itself is encouraged.

The problem is that we become too attached to some aspect of ourselves or our partners. You come to see them in some way. You get attached to how they dress or they get attached to how you cut your hair. And then you change or they change and the other feels grief (yes, grief!) for the old ways.

We have to be able to let it all go. Let go of your old ways and embrace trying something new. Let go of your partner's old ways and encourage them to try something new. But you really liked the old way, you say. That's nice. But time moves on. Maybe the new way will be even better. Or not. Maybe you or they will go back to some older styles. That's fine too. The point is to not become attached.

Expression is transient. LIFE is evolving and transient. Just flow. Flow in your expression. Flow in your partner's expression. Allow space for all of that to expand and become more wonderful than before.

Allowing that evolution loses you nothing. There is not really any loss there. Your partner's previous expression is always a part of your past experience, and that makes room for new enjoyable expression.

More than that, your encouragement of their growth, and their encouragement of yours, is a point of connection for you both. It deepens the connection, and makes it stronger. There is only good here.

Kathryn Colleen, PhD RMT

# Purpose, Wisdom And Oneness

The next stop on your journey of connecting to your partner is the third eye chakra, located just above the eyes and nose. The third eye represents higher perception, intuition, purpose and inspiration. Connecting to your partner's higher perception, intuition, purpose and inspiration includes:

- Understanding and supporting their purpose,

- Creating a shared vision of your future together,

- Encouraging and appreciating their natural intuition, and

- Seeing their divine light.

# Understanding And Supporting Their Purpose

We each have a purpose in this life. It is often suggested that we are here to first learn something and then to give back by giving a gift that we brought with us for humanity. We all have natural gifts. Your purpose is to share your gift. Figuring out what that gift is and how to share it exactly, is really quite challenging. It's not nearly as obvious as you think it should be, until you figure it out. Then it is then most obvious thing in the world.

Over time, you and your partner will each find your purpose. Maybe you have several different purposes over the course of your life. The important thing is to support your partner's purpose, no matter what it is.

If their purpose is to be an amazing chef, that's pretty easy to support. But what if their purpose is to help people in war zones? What if their purpose takes them away from you sometimes? It has to be OK. Because to hold them back from their purpose is to make them miserable, and a good partner does not want to see their love in misery.

Meanwhile, you are discovering your own purpose. And your partner can support you in that as well. Carrying out your purpose fills your soul. When you are together, you will have that much more to give each other.

Here are some fun exercises to help you both find your purpose. My best advice would be to try them all until you find one that works for you and/or you spot a pattern or connection in the results... here they are, reprinted and paraphrased from the book, *Purna Asatti*...

## Free Flow Writing

Get a bank piece of paper or pull up a blank note on your phone or computer (whichever will allow you to get ideas down the fastest). Start by asking yourself, "What is my purpose?," or, "What is my mission in life?"

Then, write whatever comes to mind. Just start listing and keep listing until you get to something that makes you tear up. An emotional response is the key to spotting the right answer.

## Intersections

Write down four separate lists: (1) What you are good at, (2) What you enjoy, (3) What the world needs and (4) what you can get paid for. Your purpose or mission in life is what lies at the intersection of these four things.

Now, I kind of don't necessarily agree with the idea that your purpose in life is necessarily linked to an income. I suspect that the idea of being able to be paid for it suggests that it has value to society at large. I would focus more on that concept - that it has value to society. If, however, you are doing this exercise because you want a new career and you are not yet financially free, then, yes, I would include the getting paid part.

## What Have You Always Done?

In this exercise, you look back from childhood until now and ask yourself what have you always done, when nobody is looking, when you are not getting paid for it, etc. What MUST you do just because you cannot imagine not doing it? What activities are simply at the core of your being and always have been?

**Skills Assessment**

Ask people you trust (and who would tell you honestly), like your partner, to list the skills that you are really really really good at. Which of your best skills gives you joy? How can you double down on and possibly combine those skills?

**The Simon Sinek Method**

Call a small number of your closest friends (people that have known you a long time). For each, ask them, "Why are you my friend?". They may have a hard time and need to think about that to really get to the heart of it. But keep digging and they will eventually have an epiphany about how you make them FEEL or some other thing that you do for their INTERNAL self. This is the value that you bring to humanity. How can you leverage that into a purpose, mission or vocation?

## The Tony Robbins Method

Tony Robbins has lots of very insightful methods for everything and this is no exception. It goes like this... When you were very young (3-5 years old), what did you want to be when you grew up? WHY? Then, when you were a teenager, what did you want to do for a career? WHY? Then, when you were in your twenties, what did you want to do for a career? WHY? Thirties?.... keep going until you reach your present age. Then, focus on all the WHYs. What is the pattern? Can you combine them into one purpose, mission or vocation?

## Sit Down, Shut Up & Listen

In this method, you simply ask for the answer and it is delivered to you. This is also called mediation, prayer or as Jesse Elder puts it, Cosmic Google. It is wonderfully effective, although it takes some practice. Find a quiet place where you can be alone and will be guaranteed to be undisturbed for a period of time... let's say 15-60 minutes. Put your phone on airplane mode and get all your typical distractions as far away from you as possible.

Sit down. Quiet your mind by listening to the silence intently. Ask your question; in this case, "What is my mission?," or, "What is my purpose?". Wait patiently for the answer and write it down exactly as you heard it - do not stop to interpret it. And don't dismiss it. Think about how it fits in with what you found from the other methods.

Let me remind you that your result is not going to look exactly like anything you have seen before, so if it looks like that, you need to be more specific and carry out your mission in a more unique way, by a new method, etc. Get creative and don't let society's rules steer you away from your true answer.

## Creating A Shared Vision Of Your Future Together

Once you have an idea of your purpose, create a shared vision of a future that excites you both and has space for you both to grow, explore interests, and fulfill your purposes in joint support. Your future could look like anything you want. Don't feel like you have to adhere to any menu of options that other people think is right. Here are some questions to get you started...

- What do you want your finances to look like? Do you want to be financially independent?

- Do you love to work traditional jobs?

- If you didn't have to work, what would you do with your time, after all the partying and bucket list items were done? Why?

- What does your ideal day look like? Why?

- If you could live anywhere, where would you live? What town or country? What kind of house or apartment? Why?

- What would you need to do now, to make that life happen?

It's OK if your ideal life plan takes some years to make happen. You may need to get out of debt and save up to be financially independent. That can take time. You might have children to factor into the mix. You might be ideally happy right where you are, doing what you are doing right now.

You might also have very different ideas of what ideal life looks like. In that case, create a shared vision that accommodates you both. For example, suppose that one of you wants to travel and the other does not. There is nothing wrong with just one of you traveling. You can support each other, traveler and homebody alike, without resentment or attachment. If you have done the other homework thus far, then you each have a solid strength of self and will not be intimated or threatened by each other's preferences.

Let's take another example. Suppose that one of you likes your job a lot and wants to keep working while the other wants to retire and chase a life long dream of volunteering within a children's charity. Why not? There should be no resentment if you are in agreement on that shared vision, and no guilt either. If you are each doing what you really want to do, resentment and attachment do not enter the equation. It is only when one of you is held back or holding yourself back that resentment and attachment cause problems.

## Encouraging Intuition And Seeing Their Divine Light

We all have a natural intuition. We might call it a gut feeling, or a vibe. You may have noticed that it has never led you astray. Just like a muscle, your intuition gets stronger with use.

Learning to listen to your intuition is a skill that you can continually improve. Practice recognizing the difference between being compelled from a place of intuition versus a fear-driven impulse. One way to tell the difference is to locate where you feel it in your body. Intuition is often felt in the heart or gut, while impulse is felt in the brain or solar plexus.

Even as you work on honing your own intuition, you can encourage and appreciate your partner's intuition. When you affirm their intuition on a decision, you are helping them make it stronger. Your combined intuition on any issue is a powerful advisor. So encourage each other to listen to your gut.

If intuition is divine guidance, then the divine is resident in your partner, and in you, naturally. In each of us is the spark of the divine. The divine light. Sometimes, when your love is happy, they just seem to glow. See the light inside that radiates through them.

Try this... See them as an angel, god or goddess. What if they were? How would you treat them differently? Pretend for a while that they are, in fact, an angel here on earth, or a god or goddess incarnate. Treat them that way and see what happens.

Every religion in the world says, in one way or another, that The divine is in us; in our hearts, guiding us along, part of every cell of our bodies, and so forth. Think about that. Every cell of your being carries the divine light. That's a lot of responsibility.

You are inherently divine. And your partner is inherently divine. You are each and together the divine, walking this earth, learning about itself. If you treat yourself as sacred, you will act a little differently. If you treat your partner as sacred, they will respond by being exactly that.

Sometimes it is easier to see the divine light in someone else. So in this one case, start by seeing it in your partner and have them see it in you. That will make it easier to see it in yourselves.

## Oneness And Transcendence

Our last stop along your journey of connection as a couple is the crown chakra, often associated with wisdom, oneness and transcendence. Let's take those one at a time. Connecting to your partner's wisdom is about appreciating their intellect and all they have learned from their life experiences. There is a lot you can both learn from each other. It might be as simple as a useful headline one of you shares, or some useful information you found.

Often it is wisdom in the form of perspective when you need it the most. When one of you is having a hard day, or in danger of an emotional decision, the other can offer perspective and advice that is right on target. When your partner offers wisdom, do not dismiss it. Listen, consider it, and offer them appreciation for it.

That being said, don't offer wisdom if you don't have it. So, where is the fine line between being a source of wisdom and an insufferable know it all? If you have done your homework thus far, your intuition is getting better by the day. Let your intuition tell you when to offer your thoughts and experience.

Otherwise, let your partner ask for your wisdom before offering it. It is a delicate balance for sure.

Talk with your partner about how you think the world works and how you think the divine works. You don't need any special qualifications to discuss your thoughts on life and the divine. All humanity has a valid perspective. Don't let this topic be off limits just because you don't have all the answers. It is enough to just have some good questions.

Feel at one with each other. See how you are the same. You are both just people; pieces of the divine light on this journey together, finding your purpose, making your way. Can you see aspects of yourself in them? Can you see aspects of your partner in you?

Remember the eye gazing and snuggling from before? Use that here. Now, when you look in your partner's eyes, feel how you are the same. Feel what it is like to be them. For an extra challenge, Feel what it is like to be them, feeling what it is like to be you. Most importantly, feel your CONNECTION.

Experience shared transcendence by opening to each other and connecting completely along all of these aspects that you have now developed. You have come a very long way.

You began first by establishing and building trust and safety. You learned to ground each other. You connected through sexuality, compassion, love, truth, expression, intuition, purpose, and now wisdom. All of these elements meld together to create complete connection between you and your partner.

It can feel like a lot to maintain. But you will find that all the little things become habit: looking them in the eyes, making them feel safe and grounded, offering compassion, rewarding them when they express their truth and themselves, and so on. Before you know it, it all becomes second nature. Love becomes natural and easy. Love becomes fun and playful. And as always, Love = Joy + Awe + Gratitude.

Make Love Every Day

Kathryn Colleen, PhD RMT

# All About Love - Frequently Asked Questions Answered

## The Capacity To Love And Be Loved

We all want to be loved; and we all want to love someone else. Unfortunately, sometimes, the people we love do not seem to love us very much or at all, in return. It's even worse when they claim to love you but their actions clearly speak otherwise. They insist that they love you, but their actions and/or words demonstrate that they do not. It becomes confusing and painful. Do they or don't they?

They do, to the limited extent that they can. The large majority of the time (unless it's a one night stand or random stranger), your family, spouse, long term love interests, children, etc really do actually love you. However - and this is critical - their capacity to love you is limited by their capacity to love themselves. That is, they can only love you to the extent that they love themselves.

Someone who hates or despises themselves cannot love you in the way you probably expect them to. They are limited in what they can be for you. Likewise, someone who generally likes themselves but does not really love themselves can be a friend or acquaintance to you but cannot give you the kind of romantic love or parental love that you deserve. Relationships (family or romantic) will appear to work well in good times and when you are well matched on your capacity to love.

Over time, we each evolve at our own pace and (generally) our capacity to love ourselves and others grows. As the differences between your capacity to love and that of those around you become apparent, you may misinterpret their lack of capacity as not loving you. Looking at their not-loving actions, there is plenty of proof. Then you might think they are lying. And while some certainly are, most are not lying. They really do think, feel and believe that they love you. But they are not fully capable of loving you.

They lack the capacity and the skills. It's just like when a child with a bike thinks and feels they are a daredevil as they jump over small obstacles in the street. They are... but their capacity to dare is a skill set that has not developed terribly far. Evel Knievel on the other hand, had a very developed sense of daring and the skills to match. Similarly, you can develop your own capacity to love and the skills to go with it.

The lesson is this: to assess what type of relationship and/or boundaries you should have with someone, consider how much they really love themselves. Consider their capacity to love versus the kind of loving relationship that you need or want.

While you are at it, take a look in the mirror. Is there any self-loathing you need to work on so that you can have the capacity to love in the way that others deserve?

As always, you cannot change others so work instead on yourself.

# Why We Seek Love And How To Know If Love is "Real"

This is as applicable to your romantic interests as it is to your parents and family. Why are so many people bent on acquiring something that seems so fragile and fleeting?

To be human is to crave real, unconditional love. We chase it all of our lives. When we are young, what we are really chasing is validation. We seek validation of who we think we are in that moment. We seek validation that we are worthy of love. We seek validation that we are "good enough". Good enough for what? Good enough to be loved.

Love appears to be ephemeral. You had it. Then it was gone. It evaporated. Because it was not love. What you had was attachment or conditional love. More on that in a minute. After a few experiences of seeming to have love in our lives and then watching it evaporate, we start to think this thing called real love does not exist.

This is usually when people make a terrible mistake and settle for something less than love only to end in misery and broken lives. I want to save you from that.

It's funny that with all this physical world around us that we seek something that does not have physical form. Most of us spend a period of our lives seeking physical things that we think will make us feel whole: degrees, jobs, money, houses, cars, people, titles, etc. After those things fail to bring us that fulfillment, we start to look to the intangibles like purpose and love. Ultimately, I believe that we are driven to seek love because we are driven to find ourselves. That will make more sense in a moment.

How can you be sure that someone truly loves you?

There are several nuances here. Each of us has a capacity to love. Some, depending on what stage they are in, are only capable of attachment. As we grow and evolve, that capacity to love gets bigger and more capable. We move through a stage where we have the capacity for conditional love, and we keep growing until we have the capacity for divine love.

Divine love is unconditional and what most of us think of when we say true love.

When someone claims to love you, they may really feel that they do. The key is to assess their capacity to love. That is, see if you can figure out if their love is attachment, conditional love or divine (unconditional) love.

Here is a guide...

## Attachment

Attachment feels like them pulling you in towards them. Pay attention to how you feel in your gut when you are around them. If you can feel the energy in your body, it will feel like them pulling you in. They are grasping for you. You fill a need for them. They are afraid of losing you. They tend to your needs out of fear of loss. They may try to control you. If they have expectations of you, this is attachment. If they say, "If you love me, you would...", this is attachment, not love.

If they are currently spending a lot of time in Stages Three, Four or Five, you almost certainly have attachment here. That is not to say they don't love you to the extent that they can. They just don't have the capacity for unconditional love yet. Attachment is all they can muster. They may be a wonderful person (or not). But we are all just here on this journey, going around this cycle of development. Don't hold it against them. See their humanity, and feel compassion for the fact that you are in this journey together. We are all just human.

With time, as they evolve, they may find the capacity for real, true love (the unconditional kind). Are they worth the time and effort? We all are, but you cannot (and should not) force them to evolve if they don't truly want to. Should you offer them a chance to evolve? No. That is putting a condition on your love. They may try out of fear of losing you. And any choice made out of fear multiplies that fear. Be kind. Don't interfere with their journey unless they specifically ask for your help on their own.

## **Conditional Love**

Conditional love can look a lot like the divine love we are all looking for. It can be very confusing. They say they love you. And it is reasonable to assume that they DO love you, to the extent that they CAN. As an example, our parents love us unconditionally, at first. No matter how much you cry and make messes, they just love you. But, as Tony Robbins says, try that when you're forty. At some point around two years old, their love becomes conditional on you acting the right way, getting good grades, taking on certain careers, fulfilling certain family expectations, etc.

There is that word again - EXPECTATIONS. Do they ever withdraw their Love? The withdrawal of love feels terrible. We would do anything to get it back. So we try to meet their conditions. Many marriages are this way too. Although there is a level of caring here, sometimes quite a lot of caring, this is not really the true love you are looking for. It can get confusing because they say they love you but sometimes they withdraw their love when they are angry or in a bad mood or when you did not meet their expectations. They may not treat you nicely.

If they love you, how could they be mean to you? Their love is conditional. They love you to the extent that they can, and this is it... for now. Parents, as an example, sometimes (if you are lucky) move from conditional love to unconditional love once you are off on your own and no longer spending their money. That is, once you don't need them for anything and they do not need you for anything. But that assumes they have evolved to at least Stage Eight.

## Divine Love

Ah, that perfect unconditional love. THIS is what we are all chasing; real true love like it was sent down from heaven. Real love feels like it is pouring OUT of them and into you. It makes your heart feel bigger, like it is radiating out of you at the thought of them. Real love has no expectations. You don't need them for anything. You are complete unto yourself. And they don't need you for anything. They are complete unto themselves.

You CHOOSE to be around each other because the love and the joy multiplies when you are near each other. They never withdraw their love from you, even if they feel angry. They are always kind. They never call you names or yell at you. They never make threats. They never set conditions. They do not belittle you or make you feel bad about yourself. They lift you up. They encourage you.

But they don't lie to you, even to make you feel better. They call you out when you are fooling yourself or about to do something detrimental. But they do it kindly. You can feel their love, radiating out of them all the time, no matter the situation... unconditionally.

This type of love is so incredibly rare. You can count them on one hand over a lifetime. If you have someone in your life (a family member or romantic interest) who has the capacity to love you like this, revel in it! Work to evolve your own capacity to return that love. I swear that this kind of love is so tangible it has weight and substance.

## The Capacity To Love And Be Loved

Another way you can tell if someone has the capacity to love you unconditionally, is to see how much they love themselves. Our capacity to love others is limited to our capacity to love ourselves. Do they really, truly love themselves? Watch them.... it takes a long time to get to a point where we really love ourselves. Most people are not there yet. The average person still does things that detriment themselves. They may regularly, knowingly sabotage themselves. They may think terrible things about themselves or put up with unhealthy situations. You get the idea. If they do not love themselves, they cannot possibly love you the way you hope they will.

That does not mean they don't care what happens to you. They might care quite a lot. They might enjoy their time with you immensely. The relationship might be a fine idea as a friendship, or family relationship, if you enjoy that time together too. Most of your "love" relationships (friends and family) will be like that and can be very fulfilling.

## Looking In The Mirror

While you assess others for their capacity to love you, don't forget to look in the mirror. What is your capacity to love yourself? You can work to evolve that to the point of unconditional love for yourself so that you will have the capacity to love others unconditionally.

This happens naturally as you evolve through the stages on the cycle of development. Work to evolve yourself and you will naturally come to love yourself fully and truly. Then you will have the kind of love you seek. Guaranteed. You must love yourself unconditionally before you can offer that to (or seek that from) someone else.

As usual, life has a bit of a twisted sense of humor. You will get that unconditional love once you don't really need it, because you are providing it for yourself. The crazy thing is... once you come to love yourself this way... the river of your life will quickly deliver someone into your life that can love you that way too. And you can be that for them. And life is freaking beautiful. I speak from experience. It is real.

In fact, I am starting to believe that unconditional love is one of very few things that actually IS real.

I have so much compassion for you in this experience. The confusion can be so frustrating. But you are so very worthy of real love ... first from yourself, and then from others. Don't ever doubt that.

## Real Love = Joy, Awe And Gratitude

I am often asked about how to recognize real love. We have just detailed the complex answer. Here I want to share a simpler test. Suppose someone claims to love you. Or maybe you think you love someone else. Let's find out!

Real love is a combination of three things: joy, awe and gratitude.

Let's start with the case where you think you love someone. First, you must ask yourself if you really know this person. Do you really see their truth? Or are you just projecting what you want them to be? If you know their truth then you can test your love like this:

**Do you feel joy?** Does the fact they exist at all in this world make you smile? Regardless of their actions, do you feel joy that they exist?

**Next, do you feel awe?** Do you feel amazed at the fact that someone like that exists in this world? Do you feel awe at certain aspects of their personality?

**Lastly, do you feel gratitude?** Do you feel gratitude for the fact that they exist in this world? Do you express your gratitude to them? Do you feel gratitude for all they do for you?

If you feel joy, awe and gratitude when you think about them, then what you are feeling is divine unconditional love.

Now let's turn that around. Suppose someone loves YOU. Let's find out. Is it unconditional love, conditional love or something else like lust or infatuation?

**Does your mere existence bring them joy?** Do they take joy in seeing you happy? Do they take joy in supporting your independent path in this world?

**Are they in awe of you?** Do they express awe in some aspects of your personality or skill sets?

**Do they feel and express gratitude?** Are they thankful that you exist at all in this world? Do they express gratitude for the things you do for them?

If so, this is real unconditional love! Enjoy!

Now sometimes, people, may feel things that they do not express. They may feel joy, awe and gratitude but fail to express it. In these cases, you may catch them looking at you and smiling with that sheepish joy/amazement look.

Take a look at your own feelings and how much of them you express. Express your joy. Express your amazement and awe. And certainly express your gratitude.

The best part is, you can express joy, awe and gratitude to anyone, anytime, even if you are shy to express love specifically. When you express your own joy, awe and gratitude, it makes people feel wonderful and that makes you feel wonderful too. Expressing these qualities creates connection.

Now, what if you realize that what you thought was unconditional love, is not? Examine it. Is it conditional love? Are you putting conditions on your love? Is your partner putting conditions on their love?

If you find that you are the one setting conditions, you can fix that. Choose to love without conditions, no matter what they say or do. Choose to find joy, awe and gratitude. Seek the ways they give you joy. Seek the things about them that inspire awe. And express your gratitude to them for what they do. See the divine light in your partner and it will grow.

If your partner is the one setting conditions, then you have a choice to make. Stay or leave. If the relationship is abusive, you should definitely leave in a safe way. If the relationship is fixable, you might want to try and fix it.

First, break the cycles within your relationship by expressing your joy, awe and gratitude for the other person. See how they naturally respond. If more change is needed, ask them to do the same. Express that you would like to be more deeply connected to them. See where it takes you.

As always, working on yourself is the first step, even in a relationship. Be the kind of partner you want to have. Love unconditionally, and unconditional love will come to you.

## How Can I Improve My Connection To My Partner By Myself?

No worries! The answer is simple. Be the partner you want to have. Lead by example. Let me explain. You are not trying to change your partner. You are not trying to brainwash or manipulate your partner. You are only seeking deeper connection.

Not everyone is into relationship exercises. That's OK. You will find that if you just open a conversation with the right question, they will answer it. For example, you will want to start with building trust. Don't say, "babe, I want us to build trust."... that's creepy.

Looking at the trust building recommendations, you can see that discussing needs and fears is important. So ask your partner what their needs are. Get them thinking. Ask them what their biggest fears are. Then, offer support and care. Basically, do your half of each exercise. Most of the time, they will ask the same questions back to you, and seeing your example, feeling your caring and support, will naturally offer the same back to you.

If they do not reciprocate, and they leave the issue one-sided, you might have to just speak up about your needs without them asking. That's perfectly OK and in fact, I encourage it. If they detail their needs and fears, share yours too! If they do not think to support your needs, ask them specifically for what you would like them to do. For example, if you did not sleep well, you might ask them if they could put the kids to bed tonight so that you could head to bed early.

In terms of sexual exercises, there is plenty you can do on your own. When your partner notices the difference (and they will!), you can divulge your new techniques. They might then be open to more.

Even finances can be a point of deepening connection. If you are usually the money master in the house, but you want them to be more involved, just strike up a conversation asking their opinion on whatever financial thing you want to discuss. You don't need to say, "I want you to be more involved." That is scary to your partner because it is too undefined. Ask your partner specific questions, like what they think about saving for some specific thing, or do they think you should have a budget line for this or that next month.

Valuing their opinion is the key to gaining their involvement. See the difference?

The thing you want to avoid is thinking that their lack of interest in the subject means something about you or them, or the relationship. It usually does not.

You might be afraid to ask for what you need. You might be afraid that they will refuse to support you. You might be afraid to face the reality that your relationship might not be a good one. But if this relationship is not a good one, you are better off knowing sooner rather than later. Speak up. Give it a try. Never be afraid to face reality. Because the reality might be that this connection has the potential for deeply divine love. And that is worth the effort.

So be the partner you want to have. Lead by example, with patience and without judgement. Offer the love and support you crave. And don't be surprised when it is all returned ten fold.

# Finding Real Love In An Age Obsessed With Looks

We want to find someone capable of real unconditional love, but you cannot assess that until you get to know them. Looks and physical attraction are the first thing that sparks us to act and strike up a conversation. We are spiritual beings having a human experience, as the saying goes. And the human species is driven to mate with the best possible option.

The thing is, criteria for what makes the best possible option varies widely and changes over time for each of us. When we are young, physical looks tend to dominate the criteria. After all, the leading men in romance films are always handsome AND otherwise perfect. In this social media age we even see people choosing a partner based on how the Instagram pics will turn out. (This is a terrible idea).

Over time, we come to see that looks don't always mean kindness, a good heart, a quick wit, a sense of humor, protection, stability, reliability, a good parent, or other qualities that we may come to crave. That good looking guy might be super nice and a great potential partner or he might be an abusive jerk. That beautiful woman might be brilliant, kind and a good mother or she might be a high maintenance nightmare.

You are absolutely right that physical attraction is what starts off any relationship. It is the gate keeper. If you are going to find real love in the form of a life partner, you are going to have to peak their attraction first, and they will have to peak yours.

But here is a good news... Not all people are attracted to the same thing. And not all women (or men) are on the lookout for the bigger better deal. Some like the muscular type, and some prefer the pudgy tattooed dad bod. Some like skinny women, and some like women with plenty of padding. Some find intellect sexy. Some want a partner who can make them laugh. Some are looking for a partner with specific hobbies and interests. Sit outside at a cafe as the weather gets warmer, down in the city. Watch the couples walking by of all ages. You will see all kinds of combinations.

The harder question is whether those couples have real love. That depends entirely on whether each individual is capable of real love for themselves. Successful couples happen when each individual has first worked on themselves to the point that they know who they are, they like who they are, and are confident in their strengths. When you know who you are and you like who you are, that energy radiates from you and is very attractive to friends and potential partners alike.

When you are young, attention from potential partners is the foundation of your self esteem. If they like you, it validates you. If they don't, you think something is wrong with you. It's time to start validating yourself.

The key, as always, is to get to know YOU. Get comfortable and confident with YOU, and develop what you have to offer.

## Make Love Every Day

Kathryn Colleen, PhD RMT

# Useful Guided Meditations

# Connecting To Your Sexuality - Mind, Body And Energy

**Focus**

Welcome. This meditation supports the Stage Three task of connecting to your sexuality - mind, body and energy. In this task, we examine our current beliefs about our sexuality and sexuality in general, we catalog our sexual needs, and explore the energy within the body through sexuality. Your sexuality is a lot more than just your preferences. It includes your beliefs, needs, mind, body and energy. Your sexuality is a vast, varied, and rich aspect of your humanity to explore. For this meditation, we will focus on clearing the slate of old beliefs and recognizing energy within the body, from the sexual perspective.

**Posture**

Take a moment to get comfortable. You can sit or stand or lay down. It doesn't matter. You may want to close your eyes for this exploration. You will certainly want to be in a private place. This meditation may induce rather strong sensations.

Allow it to be whatever it is. For this journey, you will need the visual of your partner, if you do not currently have a partner, enjoy envisioning your ideal partner instead.

**Presence**

Take a slow deep breath. Let it out like a sigh of relief. Be at peace. You are here now. Take another slow deep breath, and this time, send it out slowly, consciously, with purpose, all the way. Be at peace. You are here now. Pause and repeat these breaths until you feel relaxed and at peace.

**Journey**

We have two goals here. First, let's focus on releasing old beliefs. We begin in the heart, where truth may be found. Focus on the heart. Breathe into it.

When you think about the concept of sexuality, what emotions do you feel? Joy, guilt, fun, shame, something else?

Do you see sexuality as inherently dirty, or pure? Sacred or base?

Ask your heart ... what beliefs about sexuality are you currently holding that no longer serve you? Explore this for a moment.

Now ask you heart... what beliefs about sexuality would you like to have instead? What new beliefs could you use to replace the old beliefs? Take a moment to list these in your mind.

Now that you have some new beliefs to learn, say them over and over to yourself.

Ask your heart... can we start over now? Can we begin with a clean slate of beliefs and add just these new ones?

You are free. The slate is clean. New beliefs are in place.

With a clean slate, we are free to explore energies within the body. We will use a combination of affirmations and body-focus. From the heart, take your attention down to the solar plexus. What do you feel there? Sensations? Emotions? Name them.

As we read the following affirmations, notice how the feelings change in the solar plexus. This is energy moving. Experience this...

You are free. You are here in this body. It is yours. You are safe in this body. It is yours. And your sexuality is yours to explore.

Place your attention now on the sacral chakra, below the navel, in the middle of the pelvis. If you are familiar with the lower dantian, it is below that.

An affirmation... This is sacred space. This is the infinite space of creation. This space is yours. You reach out from this space in connection to yourself. You reach out from this space in connection to your partner.

Place your attention now on the root chakra. This chakra is located at the perineum. Imagine energy coming down into your head, down your spine, out the root chakra and into the earth. You are a conduit for the energy.

This is the energy of connection. This is the energy of all things. This is the energy of life, and love, of your partner and of yourself.

Now reverse the direction. Pull the energy up from the earth, into the root chakra, up the spine and out the crown. Do not impede the flow. Do not keep it for yourself. All the way up and out.

What energy do you feel in the root now?

Now with each breath in, bring the energy up. And with each breath out, bring the energy down. Up. Down. Up. Down.

Imagine now that your partner is with you. Breathing together. As they breathe out, sending energy out of the root, you breathe in, taking that energy into the root and up, out of the crown.

Then you breathe out, sending energy down and out. They take that energy in through their root chakra, and up and out the crown. Experience this for a moment.

This is oneness. This is the potential of your sexuality.

**Return**

When you are ready, bring your awareness back to your heart, and then back to your surroundings. Notice how you feel. Take this feeling with you and return to it anytime you like. Better yet, take this feeling and return to it with a partner.

# Connecting To Your Internal Energy And Feelings

**Focus**

Welcome. This meditation supports the Stage Three task of connecting to your internal energy and feelings. In this task, you are asked to recognize and name emotions as you feel them, and seek the root cause. You are then asked to notice how emotions correlate with energy moving in your body. This helps you connect with the energy so that you can work with it later.

This meditation will support recognizing that energy, and how it relates to emotions, as well as finding the roots of those emotions.

You should note that understanding and exploring your emotions does not mean that you need to express every feeling you have out loud, or to anyone at all. This is for your own personal exploration and understanding.

## Posture

Take a moment to get comfortable. For this exploration, you will want to sit or lay down and close your eyes.

## Presence

Take a slow deep breath. Let it out like a sigh of relief. Be at peace. You are here now. Take another slow deep breath, and this time, send it out slowly, consciously, with purpose, all the way. Be at peace. You are here now. Pause and repeat these breaths until you feel relaxed and at peace.

## Journey

We will begin with a body scan. Place your attention inside your head. What sensations are there? Notice each breath as it fills the head. Feel the brain thinking. Take a moment to explore what you physically feel there.

What emotions are there (if any)?

All emotions are rooted in one of two things... fear or love. If you feel anger, sadness, unworthiness or another negative emotion, you are ultimately afraid of something. What are you afraid of?

If you feel joy, adventure, freedom, friendship, inspiration or another positive emotion, you are ultimately in love with something... what do you feel love for?

Let's scan down the body now. Let your attention travel down to the throat. What do you feel here? What is the root of these feelings?

Move down to the heart now, home to most of our feelings of love... What do you feel here? What is the root of these feelings?

Move down to the solar plexus now... the stomach area, home to most of our fears... What do you feel here? What is the root of these feelings?

Move down now to the lower dantian... to the gut area. You may feel an expansion as you focus on this area of the body. What do you feel here... physical sensations... emotions?

You might notice that the emotions feel different here. Was it wisdom? Grounding? A more universal kind of love? Enjoy these feelings for a moment.

**Return**

When you are ready, bring your awareness back to your heart... then to the head... then to the eyes.... and finally back to your surroundings. Notice how you feel.

Take this feeling with you and return to it anytime you like by exploring the physical and energetic sensations in your body and the emotions that go with them. When you feel an emotion, explore it to find out what you are afraid of, or what you are in love with. This will allow you to express yourself more truthfully in your relationships, and even just with yourself.

# Connecting Completely To Your Partner

**Focus**

Welcome. This meditation supports the Stage Nine task of connecting to your partner. This is a vast and years long task with many different facets. In this task, you are challenged to connect with your partner in terms of trust, safety, grounding, sexuality, strength of self, compassion, love, expression, intuition, wisdom and divine nature. That's a lot!

This meditation will support that process by helping you to focus on what you love about your partner, to see their divine nature, and to express that to them to deepen connection. You can use this meditation at any step of your couple's work to boost your connection and motivation.

**Posture**

Take a moment to get comfortable. You can sit or stand or lay down. It doesn't matter. You can close your eyes or keep them open. You can hold a picture of your beloved or close your eyes and imagine them. Do what works for you.

## Presence

Take a slow deep breath. Let it out like a sigh of relief. Be at peace. You are here now. Take another slow deep breath, and this time, send it out slowly, consciously, with purpose, all the way. Be at peace. You are here now. Pause and repeat these breaths until you feel relaxed and at peace.

## Journey

We begin the day you met. Go there now. Relive this moment. How did you feel? The excitement and potential of new love. Was it magic? Was it funny? Feel thanks for that experience.

In these early days... What was it that drew you together? What was it that put you in awe of them? What was it that gave you joy? What about them made you thankful?

Time has passed... return to the present. You have both evolved from the experience, and from the course of your lives. What now puts you in awe of them? Feel awe and amazement for them. What now gives you joy in their presence? Feel joy for them. What about them are you thankful for? Feel gratitude for them.

Imagine now a future together. Deeply connected. Trusting. Grounded. Safe. Exciting. Each of you secure in your own independent selves, walking your journeys together, reveling in each other's purpose, in constant expression of love, joy, amazement, and gratitude. Deeply and completely connected. And so it will be.

Reach out to your partner with your energy and intention. Can you see how they glow? They are the divine light itself here on this earth and you get to be a part of that. You are the divine light itself here on this earth, experiencing your own divine nature, observing your love's divine nature. Shiva and Shakti. Then divine split in two to experience reuniting again.

Look at your love. What do you see? Say it to yourself. Now say it to them.

Feel now the fullness of your heart... Your crown... your whole being lit up with love, joy, awe, gratitude. Yes. Bring this to your love and be with them.

**Return**

When you are ready, bring your awareness back to your surroundings. Notice how you feel. Take this feeling with you and return to it anytime you like. Express yourself to your partner often. Let them feel your love as joy, awe and gratitude. Allow that expression to deepen your connection.

## Make Love Every Day

# Support For Your Journey

# Questions, Answers And Additional Resources

Do you have questions about what you have read here? Go to KathrynColleen.com and send in your questions. Kathryn will answer you back as quickly as possible and may include your question on the podcast or blog.

Also at KathrynColleen.com, you will find:

- Links to the full edition of the book, *Purna Asatti*, which includes specific exercises and how-to for each task plus art and poetry for a different perspective on each stage.

- The music album, *Purna Asatti - Music For Complete Connection*, that accompanies the book.

- The podcast, *On Life And Being Human*, where many of your questions may be answered.

- Other books, albums, essays and art by Kathryn Colleen.

## About The Author

Dr. Amy "Kathryn Colleen" Messegee, PhD RMT is an American-born author, composer and artist better known for her foundational work: *Purna Asatti*, a process and practice that uses connection to self, others and every aspect of your life for managing challenges and accelerating self development.

Her summer job at 16 was doing scientific research at NASA. Before her 25th birthday she earned her Ph.D in Mathematics and was speaking to conferences on human reasoning and how to make the infinite finite. A hyper-polymath, her career has enjoyed a ride through…

- academia (as a professor of Mathematics),

- defense technology (as a Scientist, CTO, and DARPA Program Manager),

- online media (as founder of a business website and video podcast with a reach of 1.3 million),

- venture capital (advising VC firms on evaluating technologies and reading the founders for their true intent),

- private education (as founder of a local network of elite tutors and private instructors),

- and her current passion: global peace, human connection and energy work.

In each of these, the theme is always the same: aggregating seemingly unrelated perspectives to distill a new approach for accelerated results. She has published many books, hundreds of articles and papers, dozens of unique art pieces and released multiple music albums.

She is known for taking only four students each year but influences and leads thousands around the world in more than 70 countries through speaking, writing, music, art and podcasts.

She is a Reiki Master Practitioner/Teacher and is travel-proficient in nine languages which she is learning simultaneously while living out her dream of traveling the world, speaking at pop up events and aggregating insight on life, the universe and being human.

See KathrynColleen.com for more information, books, articles, music, podcasts, and resources.

# Make Love Every Day

www.ingramcontent.com/pod-product-compliance
Lightning Source LLC
Chambersburg PA
CBHW070541090426
42735CB00013B/3046